MONTEVIDEO, URUGUAY TRAVEL GUIDE 2025

Sam Bennett

TABLE OF CONTENTS

CHAPTER 1: WELCOME TO MONTEVIDEO

Situated between the Atlantic Ocean and the Río de la Plata, Montevideo is Uruguay's capital and largest city. It's a place where old-world charm meets modern vibrancy, offering travelers a perfect blend of rich history, stunning landscapes, and a warm, welcoming culture. Whether you're wandering through the cobblestone streets of Ciudad Vieja, soaking up the sun along the coastal rambla, or savoring the flavors of an authentic Uruguayan asado, Montevideo invites you to immerse yourself in its laid-back yet lively atmosphere.

Montevideo is not just another stop on your South American journey – it's a city that feels like a home away from home. Unlike the fast-paced rush of larger cities, Montevideo moves at its own rhythm, offering the best of both worlds: the bustling energy of a capital city and the relaxed pace of a beachside town. It's a city with heart, where tradition is cherished and innovation is embraced. You'll find its people—known as "montevideanos"—to be friendly and approachable, always ready to share a story, a mate (traditional tea), or a bit of local insight.

Why Visit Montevideo in 2025?

The year 2025 is particularly exciting for Montevideo. Recent renovations and new cultural initiatives have breathed new life into its historical districts and modern spaces alike. If you're someone who loves discovering cities at the perfect moment—when their character is fully developed, yet not overcrowded with tourists—then Montevideo in 2025 should be at the top of your list.

The city's natural beauty is also a major draw. Whether you're an urban explorer or someone seeking a tranquil escape, Montevideo's coastline offers breathtaking views and plenty of opportunities for outdoor adventures. The rambla, a long waterfront promenade, stretches for miles and is perfect for a morning run, evening stroll, or simply watching the sunset over the water. Montevideo's beaches, though often less talked about compared to neighboring Punta del Este, have a charm of their own. Here, the sand is golden, the vibe is relaxed, and the sea invites you to pause and take in life at a slower pace.

A Cultural Tapestry

Montevideo has a cultural heartbeat that runs deep. This is the birthplace of tango, the tango that finds its roots not just in Buenos Aires but also in the soul of Uruguay. From impromptu tango performances on the streets to lively music pouring out of the city's bars and clubs, music is in Montevideo's DNA. The city's theaters and art galleries are also flourishing, offering everything from avant-garde performances to traditional folklore shows.

And speaking of folklore, you cannot miss the deep connection Uruguayans have with their traditions. The famous Uruguayan asado—more than just a barbecue—is a social event, a chance to gather with friends and family, share stories, and savor the smoky, tender meat that has been perfected over centuries. As you journey through Montevideo, you'll soon discover that food here is a passion, and trying it is an essential part of understanding the culture.

A City of Contrasts

One of the most captivating aspects of Montevideo is its blend of the old and the new. You can find yourself exploring colonial-era buildings one moment, with their intricate iron balconies and colorful facades, and walking through sleek, modern shopping districts the next. Ciudad Vieja, the city's historic old town, is home to some of Montevideo's most iconic landmarks, such as Plaza Independencia and Teatro Solís, one of the oldest theaters in South America. But just outside this historic core, Montevideo transforms into a modern metropolis, complete with chic cafes, cutting-edge galleries, and bustling markets.

What sets Montevideo apart is its authenticity. Despite its modern growth, the city has managed to preserve its unique character. You won't find skyscrapers competing for space in the skyline; instead, you'll encounter intimate streets lined with eclectic architecture, outdoor cafes, and plenty of parks that offer an oasis of calm amidst the urban energy.

A Warm Welcome

When you arrive in Montevideo, you won't just be visiting a city—you'll be welcomed into a community. Montevideo is a place where tourists are treated like locals, where sharing a meal or a drink often leads to meaningful conversations, and where you're likely to be invited to join in on a local festivity or celebration. Whether you're here for a weekend or an extended stay, Montevideo has a way of making you feel like you've found a second home.

Montevideo in 2025 is ready to be discovered, and as you embark on this journey, you'll quickly realize that this city has a little bit of magic waiting around every corner. From its historical treasures to its modern luxuries, from its cultural riches to its natural beauty, Montevideo offers an experience that is as diverse as it is unforgettable. Welcome to Montevideo, a city where every visitor is treated like an old friend.

1.1. INTRODUCTION TO THE CITY

Montevideo is a city that feels like a secret waiting to be discovered. Located on the southern coast of Uruguay, it offers the perfect balance of historic charm and modern sophistication. With a population of just under 1.5 million people, Montevideo is large enough to offer all the comforts of a modern metropolis, yet small enough to retain a laid-back, friendly vibe that many larger cities lose over time.

The city sits along the Río de la Plata, where the river meets the Atlantic Ocean, creating a scenic waterfront that defines much of Montevideo's beauty. Its 22-kilometer-long *rambla* (promenade) is one of the city's standout features, where locals and visitors alike gather to walk, cycle, jog, or simply take in the panoramic views of the water. The sound of waves crashing against the shore is a constant companion, making the city feel both vibrant and tranquil at the same time.

Montevideo is often overshadowed by its more famous South American counterparts like Buenos Aires or Rio de Janeiro, but it's precisely this relative under-the-radar status that makes it so special. Here, you'll find the charm of a city that hasn't been overrun by mass tourism. Instead, Montevideo offers an authentic travel experience, where you can explore at your own pace and truly connect with the local culture.

A City of Diversity

Montevideo is a city of contrasts, and that's what makes it so captivating. On one hand, you have the historic heart of the city, Ciudad Vieja, where narrow, cobbled streets wind their way past colonial buildings, bustling markets, and landmarks that tell the story of the city's rich past. This is where Montevideo began, and walking through this district feels like stepping back in time. From the grandeur of Plaza Independencia, where you'll find the iconic Artigas Mausoleum, to the majestic Teatro Solís, one of the oldest theaters in the Americas, Ciudad Vieja is a testament to Montevideo's history and heritage.

On the other hand, Montevideo is also a modern, thriving city with cosmopolitan flair. In neighborhoods like Punta Carretas and Pocitos, you'll find high-end boutiques, trendy cafes, and stylish restaurants, all set against the backdrop of the city's beautiful coastline. This is where Montevideo's modern side shines, offering all the luxuries and amenities of a global city, while still maintaining its laid-back, welcoming feel.

The city's diversity is not just reflected in its architecture and neighborhoods but also in its people. Montevideo is a melting pot of cultures, a place where European influences, particularly Spanish and Italian, blend seamlessly with indigenous traditions. This mix is most evident in the city's food, music, and festivals. Montevideo is the birthplace of *candombe*, a lively Afro-Uruguayan rhythm that fills the streets during Carnival, as well as tango, which has roots here just as deep as in Buenos Aires. Throughout the year, you'll find festivals celebrating everything from local folklore to contemporary arts, making Montevideo a hub of cultural activity.

A Warm and Welcoming Atmosphere

What really sets Montevideo apart, though, is its people. Known for their friendliness and hospitality, the people of Montevideo have a strong sense of community and take pride in welcoming visitors. This is not a city where tourists feel like outsiders; instead, you'll often find yourself striking up conversations with locals at a café, joining in a spontaneous *mate* (traditional tea) session along the rambla, or being invited to an *asado* (barbecue) in someone's backyard. Montevideo feels like a city that genuinely cares about its visitors, and that warmth is something you'll notice from the moment you arrive.

This atmosphere is deeply connected to the city's culture of *mate*, a communal drink that Uruguayans share with friends, family, and even strangers. You'll often see people carrying their thermos and mate cups, ready to offer a sip to anyone they meet. It's more than just a drink; it's a symbol of togetherness, a way of slowing down and enjoying the moment with those around you.

The Perfect Blend of Relaxation and Adventure

Montevideo is the kind of city that offers something for everyone. If you're the type of traveler who loves to explore history and culture, you'll find endless opportunities to dive into the city's rich past. Whether it's visiting the National History Museum or taking a walking tour of Ciudad Vieja, there's always something new to learn about Uruguay's capital.

For those seeking relaxation, the city's beaches are a haven. From the bustling Pocitos Beach, where locals gather to sunbathe and swim, to the quieter stretches of sand further along the coast, Montevideo's beaches are ideal for unwinding. And because the city is so walkable, you're never far from a quiet park or a beautiful viewpoint to pause and enjoy the scenery.

But Montevideo is also a great destination for adventure seekers. Whether it's cycling along the rambla, exploring the city's green spaces like Parque Rodó, or even venturing outside the city for day trips to the scenic wine country or nearby Colonia del Sacramento, there's plenty to keep you on the move.

A City for All Seasons

One of the best things about Montevideo is that it's a great destination year-round. Its temperate climate means that even in winter, the weather remains mild and pleasant, perfect for exploring the city's parks, beaches, and markets. Summer, of course, is the ideal time to visit if you're looking to enjoy the city's beaches, open-air concerts, and festivals. But no matter when you choose to visit, Montevideo offers a welcoming atmosphere, vibrant culture, and countless experiences that will make you fall in love with the city.

In Montevideo, every corner has a story, every street feels alive with possibility, and every moment is a chance to connect with the city's rich heritage and warm-hearted people. As you begin your journey here, you'll quickly discover that Montevideo is not just a place to visit – it's a place to experience.

1.2 WHY VISIT IN 2025

Montevideo is already a gem of South America, but in 2025, it's set to shine brighter than ever before. Whether you're a seasoned traveler or someone looking for their next adventure, 2025 is the perfect time to experience all that this dynamic city has to offer. From cultural festivities to exciting new developments, the city is primed to give you an unforgettable travel experience. Here's why Montevideo should be at the top of your travel list in 2025.

A Year of Celebration and Growth

The year 2025 marks several milestones for Montevideo, making it an exceptionally exciting time to visit. The city has been undergoing a cultural renaissance in recent years, and 2025 is when it all comes together. Historic landmarks have been restored, new spaces have been opened to the public, and an array of festivals and events are planned to celebrate Uruguay's rich cultural heritage.

One of the biggest reasons to visit Montevideo in 2025 is the city's planned Bicentennial celebrations. This momentous occasion will be marked by special events, parades, and exhibitions that will immerse you in the history and identity of Uruguay. From lively street performances in Ciudad Vieja to grand concerts at the iconic Teatro Solís, the celebrations will highlight everything that makes Montevideo such a unique and vibrant city.

Montevideo's waterfront, known as the *rambla*, has also seen major improvements, with new parks and public spaces designed to make the most of the city's stunning coastal location. These enhancements have created more opportunities for outdoor recreation, with designated areas for walking, cycling, and even outdoor concerts and festivals.

So, whether you're an active traveler who enjoys running along the coastline or someone who loves sitting by the water with a good book, the revamped *rambla* is the perfect place to relax and soak in the city's relaxed pace.

Rich Cultural Offerings

Montevideo has always been a cultural hub, and in 2025, its cultural calendar is packed with events you won't want to miss. The city is known for its rich music, dance, and art scenes, with tango and *candombe* rhythms setting the tone for many of its lively festivals.

Carnival, which is already one of the most colorful and joyful celebrations in Uruguay, promises to be extra special in 2025. This vibrant event is a month-long party that brings the entire city to life with parades, street performances, and concerts. *Candombe*, a musical tradition with African roots, takes center stage during Carnival, filling the streets with the sound of drums and energetic dance performances. For visitors, Carnival offers a unique opportunity to see

Montevideo at its most joyful and to join in the festivities alongside the locals.

In addition to Carnival, Montevideo will also host a series of art exhibitions, film festivals, and live music events that showcase the city's thriving creative community. Teatro Solís, one of the oldest theaters in South America, is set to host a number of special performances throughout the year, featuring everything from classical opera to contemporary dance. Whether you're a culture enthusiast or just someone looking to experience something new, Montevideo in 2025 has an event or performance to capture your imagination.

An Emerging Culinary Destination

While Montevideo may not be as well-known as other South American cities for its food, that's changing rapidly—and 2025 is the year to taste it for yourself. The city's culinary scene has experienced a renaissance in recent years, and this resurgence shows no signs of slowing down. In 2025, food lovers will find a Montevideo that's bustling with innovative restaurants, vibrant food markets, and a burgeoning wine scene that's putting Uruguay on the global map.

Uruguayan cuisine is rooted in tradition, with the *asado*—a communal barbecue—being at the heart of it all. But in 2025, chefs in Montevideo are reinterpreting these classic flavors with a modern twist, blending old-world techniques with contemporary trends. The Mercado del Puerto, a lively food market in the heart of the city, is a must-visit spot for anyone wanting to taste the authentic flavors of Montevideo. Here, you'll find stalls serving up everything from sizzling meats to freshly caught seafood, all paired with Uruguay's finest wines.

Speaking of wine, Uruguay's reputation as a wine-producing country has grown significantly in recent years, and 2025 is the perfect time to explore the region's vineyards. The nearby wine regions, just a short drive from Montevideo, are offering expanded tours and tastings, allowing visitors to sample Uruguay's signature varietal, Tannat, alongside other world-class wines. Wine lovers will appreciate the intimate, boutique feel of Uruguay's wineries, which offer a relaxed and personal tasting experience that larger wine regions often lack.

Sustainable and Eco-Friendly Tourism

Montevideo is committed to sustainability, and 2025 brings a range of new initiatives that make it easier for visitors to enjoy the city while minimizing their environmental impact. The city has invested in green spaces, eco-friendly public transportation, and sustainable tourism practices that prioritize the health of the environment and the well-being of local communities.

For those looking to travel responsibly, Montevideo offers plenty of eco-friendly accommodation options, from boutique hotels that use renewable energy to locally-owned guesthouses that support sustainable farming practices. The city's push towards sustainability extends to its culinary scene as well, with farm-to-table restaurants popping up across town, offering fresh, locally sourced ingredients that reflect the best of Uruguayan agriculture.

Outdoor enthusiasts will also appreciate Montevideo's commitment to preserving its natural beauty. The city's parks and beaches are cleaner than ever, and eco-tourism activities like kayaking, bird-watching, and hiking have been expanded to give visitors a closer look at the region's diverse ecosystems.

For those who want to explore beyond the city, Montevideo serves as the perfect gateway to Uruguay's many natural wonders, including the picturesque countryside and pristine nature reserves.

A City on the Rise

Montevideo in 2025 is a city on the rise, ready to be explored and experienced by travelers from all walks of life. Whether you're looking to dive into the city's rich cultural heritage, indulge in its emerging culinary scene, or simply enjoy a laid-back escape by the water, Montevideo offers something for everyone. With its perfect blend of history, modernity, and natural beauty, the city has never been more vibrant—or more welcoming.

By choosing to visit Montevideo in 2025, you're not just visiting a city, but becoming part of a special moment in its history. You'll experience a city that is proud of its past, excited about its future, and eager to share its many treasures with the world. If you're looking for an unforgettable travel experience, Montevideo is waiting for you with open arms.

CHAPTER 2: GETTING TO MONTEVIDEO

Montevideo, the capital of Uruguay, is nestled along the southern coast of South America, offering a seamless blend of modernity, rich culture, and coastal beauty. But before you dive into the city's unique experiences, let's talk about the journey itself—how to get there. Getting to

Montevideo in 2025 is more convenient than ever, whether you're coming from a neighboring country or flying from across the globe. With an expanding network of flights, efficient border crossings, and well-connected transport links, arriving in this vibrant city is as exciting as the adventures that await you.

When you're planning your trip to Montevideo, it's not just about booking a flight; it's about setting the tone for your journey. How you arrive plays a crucial role in shaping your first impressions of this dynamic city. Let's take a look at the different ways you can reach Montevideo and what you need to know before you arrive.

Flights to Montevideo

For most international travelers, flying into Montevideo will be the quickest and most convenient option. The city's main airport, Carrasco International Airport (MVD), is located just a short 20-minute drive from the city center, making it easy to hit the ground running as soon as you land. Over the years, the airport has expanded its reach, now offering direct flights from major cities across Europe, North America, and South America, making Montevideo more accessible than ever before.

Flying into Carrasco International is more than just a simple transit—Uruguay takes pride in its welcoming atmosphere, and you'll feel that warmth from the moment you step off the plane. The airport is modern and efficient, offering an array of services to make your arrival as smooth as possible. Whether you need to pick up a local SIM card, exchange currency, or grab a quick snack after a long flight, you'll find everything you need at the airport.

If you're traveling from within South America, several low-cost airlines offer frequent flights to Montevideo, making it a breeze to hop over from Buenos Aires, São Paulo, Santiago, or other nearby hubs. Regional flights are affordable, and with Uruguay's proximity to Argentina and Brazil, you can easily include Montevideo in a multi-country itinerary.

Arriving by Land or Sea

For those already traveling in South America, getting to Montevideo by land or sea is another great option. One of the most popular routes is the ferry service from Buenos Aires, Argentina. This scenic ride across the Río de la Plata is a travel experience in itself. With comfortable seating, onboard amenities, and stunning views of the river, the ferry journey offers a relaxing and picturesque way to arrive in Uruguay. Depending on the service you choose, you can reach Montevideo in as little as three hours.

Once you arrive at the port in Montevideo, you'll be right in the heart of the city, with the historic Ciudad Vieja just steps away from where you disembark. It's the perfect way to start your exploration of Montevideo, with the city's colonial architecture, vibrant street life, and famous Mercado del Puerto waiting to greet you.

For overland travelers, Montevideo is well-connected to the rest of Uruguay and its neighboring countries. Bus services from Argentina, Brazil, and Paraguay are frequent, affordable, and comfortable, with long-distance coaches offering everything from reclining seats to onboard Wi-Fi. Traveling by bus gives you the chance to see more of the South American landscape, with scenic routes taking you through

rolling hills, rural towns, and lush countryside before arriving in the bustling capital.

What to Expect Upon Arrival

Regardless of how you choose to get to Montevideo, one thing is for sure: you'll be welcomed with open arms. Uruguay is known for its friendly, laid-back vibe, and that's reflected in the way travelers are greeted. Immigration and customs processes are typically straightforward, with minimal hassle. In 2025, Uruguay has simplified its entry requirements, and for most visitors, visas are not required for stays of up to 90 days. Make sure your passport is valid for at least six months beyond your arrival date, and you'll be good to go.

Transportation from the airport or ferry terminal into the city is easy and reliable. Taxis and ride-sharing services are readily available, and for those on a budget, local buses provide an affordable way to reach the city center. If you're renting a car, the roads are well-marked and easy to navigate, and you'll find that Montevideo's traffic is relatively light compared to other capital cities in the region.

Once you've arrived, it's time to settle in and get ready to explore. Montevideo's unique charm lies in its balance of old-world elegance and modern flair, and no matter how you get here, your adventure is just beginning.

2.1. FLIGHTS AND TRANSPORT OPTIONS

Montevideo is a vibrant and cosmopolitan city, and getting there has never been easier. Whether you're coming from another South American destination or flying in from halfway across the globe, the city offers a variety of flights and transport options that will suit every kind of traveler. Here's everything you need to know about your journey to Montevideo.

Flights to Montevideo: Carrasco International Airport (MVD)

Most international travelers arriving in Montevideo will land at **Carrasco International Airport (MVD),** Uruguay's largest and most modern airport. Located about 20 kilometers from the city center, Carrasco International is not just a gateway to Montevideo—it's an introduction to the country's hospitality. The sleek, contemporary design of the airport reflects the blend of modernity and warmth that you'll experience throughout your trip.

Flights into Montevideo are available from major cities across the Americas and Europe. For North American travelers, direct flights from Miami, New York, and Houston make getting to Montevideo straightforward, while connections from cities like Buenos Aires, São Paulo, Santiago, and Panama City link Montevideo with much of Latin America. European travelers can fly directly from Madrid, and connections are available from other key cities like Paris and London via neighboring hubs.

What's particularly appealing about flying into Montevideo is that the airport is highly efficient, yet not overwhelmingly busy. After a long international flight, you'll appreciate the ease with which you can move through immigration, collect your luggage, and find your way into the city. Upon arrival, the airport's services are comprehensive, offering everything from currency exchange and ATMs to cafes and car rental services.

Direct Flights or Stopovers?

While Montevideo does have a number of direct flights from international hubs, many travelers opt for stopovers in nearby cities such as Buenos Aires or São Paulo. This can be an excellent option if you want to break up your long journey and explore more of South America along the way.

If you're flying into Buenos Aires, for example, you can take a short flight or ferry across the Río de la Plata to reach Montevideo. The ferry, in particular, offers a scenic and relaxing way to begin your Uruguayan adventure. It's about a three-hour journey, and as you sail across the river, you'll get breathtaking views of both cities, setting the stage for the discoveries that lie ahead.

Transport from Carrasco International Airport to the City

Once you've touched down in Montevideo, you'll find plenty of transport options to get you from the airport to the city center. Taxis, ride-sharing services, buses, and rental cars are all readily available, and each has its own advantages depending on your travel preferences.

Taxis: Taxis are the most convenient option for travelers with luggage or those who want to head straight to their accommodation with minimal hassle. Taxis are plentiful at the airport, and you can easily spot the official airport taxis just outside the arrivals area. The journey into the city takes about 20-30 minutes, depending on traffic, and costs between $30 and $40 USD. While this is the priciest option, it's also the most direct and comfortable after a long flight.

Ride-Sharing Services: If you're familiar with apps like Uber or Cabify, you'll be glad to know that these services are available in Montevideo. They are often cheaper than taxis and provide a convenient alternative for getting into the city. Ride-sharing services can be booked through their respective apps, and you can expect a ride to the city to cost around $20-$25 USD. Just make sure to have mobile data or Wi-Fi access to book your ride when you land.

Public Buses: For budget-conscious travelers, the **public bus** is a cost-effective way to reach Montevideo's city center. Buses leave regularly from the airport and head to various parts of the city. The journey may take longer—about 45 minutes to an hour—but it's an excellent way to get your first taste of local life. Tickets cost around $2-$3 USD, making this an affordable option for solo travelers or those looking to save money. Look for buses heading to the **Tres Cruces bus terminal**, which is centrally located.

Car Rentals: If you're planning to explore beyond Montevideo during your stay, renting a car at the airport might be a great option. Several international and local car rental agencies operate at Carrasco International Airport, offering a range of vehicles to suit your needs. Driving in Montevideo is relatively straightforward, and having a car gives you the freedom to explore not just the city, but also Uruguay's stunning beaches, countryside, and nearby towns at your own pace. Just be sure to familiarize yourself with local driving regulations and parking options in the city center.

Arriving by Sea: Ferry from Buenos Aires

One of the most scenic ways to arrive in Montevideo is by taking the ferry from Buenos Aires, Argentina. The ferry ride across the Río de la Plata is not only a practical transportation option but also a beautiful journey in itself. The two main ferry companies that operate this route are **Buquebus** and **Colonia Express**, with several departures throughout the day.

The ferry ride typically takes about three hours, offering a relaxing way to enjoy the water and the view of both Montevideo and Buenos Aires. Once you arrive at the port in Montevideo, you're already in the heart of the city, making it easy to start exploring right away. The ferry is particularly popular with travelers who are combining visits to both Argentina and Uruguay, and the comfort and convenience of the service make it a memorable part of the trip.

Bus Travel: Arriving by Land

If you're traveling through South America, Montevideo is well-connected by long-distance buses. Buses from Buenos Aires, São Paulo, and other major South American cities arrive daily at Montevideo's **Tres Cruces bus terminal**, the city's central hub for intercity and international buses. Long-distance buses in this part of the world are surprisingly comfortable, often featuring reclining seats, Wi-Fi, and meal services. This is an excellent option for those looking for an affordable and scenic way to reach Montevideo.

Buses are a popular choice for travelers who enjoy the journey as much as the destination, allowing you to see more of Uruguay's rural landscapes before arriving in the city. Depending on where you're coming from, bus travel can be an adventure in itself, with plenty of opportunities to interact with locals and experience life outside of the usual tourist destinations.

No matter how you choose to get to Montevideo—whether by air, land, or sea—you'll find that the city is more accessible than ever. Each transport option offers its own unique experience, from the efficiency of modern flights to the scenic charm of a ferry ride or long-distance bus. Once you arrive, Montevideo's rich culture, friendly people, and laid-back vibe will make every moment of your journey worthwhile. The trip to Montevideo is just the beginning of an unforgettable adventure.

2.2. VISA, CUSTOMS, AND ENTRY REQUIREMENTS

Before packing your bags and heading to Montevideo, it's essential to understand the visa, customs, and entry requirements for entering Uruguay. Thankfully, for most travelers, Uruguay offers a straightforward process. Here's everything you need to know to ensure your arrival is smooth, hassle-free, and enjoyable.

Do You Need a Visa?

Uruguay has made it relatively easy for tourists from many parts of the world to visit without a visa. In fact, travelers from the **United States, Canada, the European Union, Australia, and**

many South American countries can stay in Uruguay for up to **90 days** without needing a visa. This is a great convenience for those planning a short vacation or an extended stay to explore the country. Upon arrival, you'll simply need to show your passport, which must be valid for at least six months beyond your planned departure date.

For other nationalities, a tourist visa may be required. If you're uncertain whether you need a visa, it's always a good idea to check with the **Uruguayan Embassy** or **Consulate** in your country before booking your flights. The visa application process is typically straightforward and involves providing a few basic documents like a valid passport, proof of onward travel, and sometimes evidence of accommodation or financial stability during your stay.

Once you have your visa or confirmation that you don't need one, the next step is to ensure that all other documentation is in order for your trip.

Arriving at Carrasco International Airport or any of Uruguay's ports of entry is generally a smooth process. Uruguay's customs regulations are fairly standard, and as long as you're not carrying prohibited or restricted items, you should pass through quickly. Upon arrival, you will fill out a standard **customs declaration form**, which is typically handed out during your flight.

Uruguay is quite welcoming when it comes to personal items, and travelers are allowed to bring personal belongings such as clothing, cameras, laptops, and other essential electronics without paying any duties. However, there are some limits and restrictions on specific items you may want to bring into the country.

Currency: You can bring in up to **USD 10,000** or its equivalent without declaring it. Any amount over this will need to be declared to customs upon entry.

Alcohol and Tobacco: You are allowed to bring in **4 liters of alcohol** and **400 cigarettes** (or 50 cigars) without paying duties. Be mindful of these limits to avoid extra charges.

Food: It's generally advised to avoid bringing large quantities of food, particularly fresh produce or meat, into the country. Uruguay has strict regulations on agricultural products to protect its own farming industry. Packaged snacks and processed goods are typically fine, but if you're carrying any food items, check with customs beforehand.

Medical and Vaccination Requirements

For most travelers, there are no mandatory vaccinations required to enter Uruguay. However, if you're arriving from a country with a risk of **yellow fever**, you may be asked to present proof of vaccination, so it's good to carry your **yellow fever vaccination card** if this applies to you. This is especially important if you've been traveling in parts of South America, Africa, or Asia where yellow fever is present.

Uruguay's health standards are high, and the country has a well-developed healthcare system, which is reassuring for travelers. It's a good idea to make sure your routine vaccinations (such as tetanus, measles, and hepatitis) are up to date before you travel. Additionally, purchasing **travel insurance** that covers medical expenses is highly recommended in case you need any health care during your trip.

When you arrive in Montevideo, you'll need to present the following documents to immigration officials:

Valid Passport: Your passport must be valid for at least **six months** beyond your planned departure date from Uruguay. This is an important detail that travelers often overlook, but it's crucial for entry.

Return or Onward Ticket: Uruguay requires proof that you'll be leaving the country within the allowed time frame, so make sure you have a **return ticket** or a ticket for onward travel. Immigration officers may ask to see this to ensure you're not planning an extended or unauthorized stay.

Proof of Accommodation: In some cases, you may be asked to provide proof of your accommodation in Uruguay, whether it's a hotel reservation or an address where you'll be staying (such as with friends or family).

Travel Insurance: While not an official requirement, having **travel insurance** is strongly recommended. It's better to be safe than sorry, especially when it comes to medical coverage and trip interruptions.

If you're planning to stay beyond the **90-day visa-free period**, you can apply for a **visa extension** at the **National Immigration Office** in Montevideo. The extension is typically granted for an additional 90 days, allowing you to stay in Uruguay for up to six months without needing to leave the country.

Bringing pets to Uruguay is possible, but there are some regulations to follow. You'll need to present a **veterinary certificate** proving that your pet is in good health and up to date with vaccinations, particularly **rabies**. Additionally, you may need to show proof that your pet has been treated for parasites within a certain time frame before entry. It's always a good idea to consult with the airline and the Uruguayan consulate before traveling with pets to ensure you meet all the requirements.

Navigating visa, customs, and entry requirements for Montevideo is fairly straightforward, especially if you're from a country with visa-free access to Uruguay. With the proper documentation in hand, a bit of preparation, and a smooth process at customs, your arrival in Montevideo will be hassle-free. Once you step off the plane or boat, you can focus on what really matters—exploring the charm and beauty of this incredible city and its surroundings. Safe travels!

CHAPTER 3: WHERE TO STAY IN MONTEVIDEO

Finding the perfect place to stay in Montevideo can shape your entire experience of this vibrant city. Whether you're looking for a cozy boutique hotel tucked away in a charming neighborhood, a luxurious waterfront suite with breathtaking views of the Río de la Plata, or a budget-friendly hostel that lets you connect with fellow travelers,

Montevideo offers something for every traveler's taste, style, and budget.

This chapter will guide you through the diverse array of accommodation options available across the city, each offering a unique slice of Montevideo's culture, charm, and hospitality. Choosing the right area to stay in is just as important as selecting your accommodation type—whether you want to immerse yourself in the city's historical heart, relax by the beach, or experience the buzzing nightlife.

We'll explore the best neighborhoods, from the historic **Ciudad Vieja** to the trendy **Pocitos**, and help you find the right place that matches your needs and expectations. Plus, we'll offer tips on what to look for when booking your stay, from amenities to location, ensuring that your time in Montevideo is as comfortable and memorable as possible. By the end of this chapter, you'll have a clear idea of where to base yourself, so you can enjoy everything the city has to offer, knowing you have a welcoming retreat to return to each night.

3.1. TOP HOTELS AND LUXURY STAYS

Montevideo's luxury hotels offer more than just a place to rest—they are an experience unto themselves. From the moment you step into one of these high-end accommodations, you'll be surrounded by elegance, comfort, and exceptional service that will make your stay in Uruguay's capital unforgettable. Whether you're looking for stunning ocean views, top-notch amenities, or simply a relaxing retreat, Montevideo's top hotels will cater to your every need.

For those seeking a blend of old-world charm and modern luxury, the **Sofitel Montevideo Casino Carrasco & Spa** is a top choice. This grand hotel, housed in a historic building that dates back to 1921, has been beautifully restored to its former glory. The elegant architecture transports you to another era, while the sophisticated interiors and state-of-the-art amenities ensure your stay is as comfortable as it is luxurious.

From its sprawling casino to its world-class spa, you'll find plenty to do within the hotel itself. But perhaps the most breathtaking feature is its location—right on the shores of the Río de la Plata. Guests can enjoy stunning views of the river while sipping cocktails on the terrace or dining at the hotel's acclaimed restaurant, **1921**, which serves a fusion of French and Uruguayan cuisine. Whether you're there for the casino, the spa, or simply to relax in style, Sofitel Montevideo promises an experience of pure indulgence.

Hyatt Centric Montevideo

Situated in the heart of the upscale **Pocitos** neighborhood, the **Hyatt Centric Montevideo** combines modern luxury with a prime location. This hotel is perfect for travelers who want to be close to the city's trendy shops, vibrant cafés, and beachside promenade. The rooms are sleek and contemporary, offering panoramic views of the coast or the city skyline. With large windows and bright, airy spaces, you'll wake up each morning to sunlight streaming into your room, setting the perfect tone for a day of exploration.

The Hyatt Centric also boasts a range of amenities to enhance your stay. The outdoor pool and fitness center are perfect for unwinding after a day of sightseeing, and the hotel's restaurant, **Plantado**, offers a culinary journey through local flavors with a contemporary twist. The warm and welcoming atmosphere, combined with the hotel's attention to detail, makes it a top pick for travelers looking for luxury without pretension.

For travelers seeking a more intimate and personalized luxury experience, the **Alma Historica Boutique Hotel** is a gem. Nestled in the heart of **Ciudad Vieja**, Montevideo's historic old town, this boutique hotel is a love letter to the city's rich cultural heritage. Each room is uniquely decorated, drawing inspiration from famous Uruguayan artists, writers, and musicians, giving guests a deeper connection to the local culture.

The hotel itself is a beautifully restored 20th-century mansion, combining the charm of yesteryear with modern comforts. The rooftop terrace is a standout feature, offering stunning views of the old town and the port—perfect for enjoying a sunset with a glass of Uruguayan wine. Alma Historica's commitment to personalized service ensures that every guest feels like they are being welcomed into a luxurious home away from home.

Hotel Cottage Carrasco

Located in the peaceful seaside neighborhood of **Carrasco**, the **Hotel Cottage Carrasco** offers a luxurious retreat just a short distance from the hustle and bustle of the city center. This hotel is ideal for those who want to combine a relaxing beachside stay with easy access to Montevideo's top attractions.

The rooms at Hotel Cottage are stylish and comfortable, many offering balconies with views of the ocean or the hotel's lush garden. The outdoor pool, surrounded by greenery, is a perfect spot to unwind, while the hotel's spa offers a range of treatments designed to help you relax and rejuvenate. The on-site restaurant serves up delicious local dishes, and the nearby beach is perfect for morning walks or an afternoon of sunbathing. Hotel Cottage Carrasco is all about comfort, tranquility, and luxury, making it an excellent choice for a peaceful getaway.

When choosing where to stay, consider what matters most to you during your visit. If you want to be close to the city's best shopping and nightlife, **Hyatt Centric Montevideo** puts you right in the heart of it all. If history and culture are your passions, **Alma Historica** immerses you in the spirit of the city. For a blend of beachside relaxation and classic luxury, **Hotel Cottage Carrasco** and **Sofitel Montevideo** both offer stunning views, world-class amenities, and a taste of Uruguay's rich heritage.

Regardless of which luxury stay you choose, Montevideo's top hotels offer more than just a bed for the night—they provide an experience that enhances your visit to the city. From gourmet dining and indulgent spas to breathtaking views and attentive service, these hotels ensure that your time in Montevideo will be as comfortable and memorable as possible.

3.2. BUDGET AND MID-RANGE ACCOMMODATIONS

Montevideo is not just a destination for luxury travelers; it also offers a wide range of budget-friendly and mid-range accommodations that ensure you don't have to break the bank to enjoy a comfortable and memorable stay. Whether you're a backpacker seeking a cozy hostel, a family looking for an affordable hotel, or a solo traveler wanting something clean, central, and reasonably priced, Montevideo's budget and mid-range accommodations have you covered.

While these places may not come with the extravagant amenities of high-end hotels, they often make up for it with charm, convenience, and a warm, welcoming atmosphere. Many of these accommodations are located in prime areas of the city, so you can still enjoy easy access to Montevideo's main attractions without overspending on your stay. Here's a look at some of the best options across the city.

If you're looking for something that combines the social atmosphere of a hostel with the comfort and privacy of a hotel, **Circus Hostel & Hotel Montevideo** is a fantastic option. Located in the heart of **Ciudad Vieja**, this spot is perfect for travelers who want to be close to Montevideo's historic center without paying premium hotel prices.

Circus offers both dorm rooms for budget-conscious backpackers and private rooms for travelers seeking more comfort and privacy. The rooms are clean, modern, and come with all the essentials, while the communal spaces, like the cozy lounge and shared kitchen, make it easy to meet fellow travelers. What sets Circus apart is its laid-back vibe, friendly staff, and its unbeatable location—just steps away from Montevideo's famous **Plaza Independencia** and the **Solis Theatre**. This makes it a great base for exploring the city's culture, nightlife, and historic sites.

Punto Berro Hostel

Another excellent choice for budget travelers is **Punto Berro Hostel**, which has locations in both

Pocitos and **Ciudad Vieja**, two of Montevideo's most popular neighborhoods. The Pocitos branch is ideal if you want to be close to the beach, while the Ciudad Vieja location places you right in the heart of the city's historic district.

At Punto Berro, the emphasis is on creating a social, friendly atmosphere. The hostel organizes regular activities such as barbecues, city tours, and movie nights, so it's easy to meet fellow travelers. The accommodations range from shared dorms to private rooms, all of which are affordable and comfortable. If you want to stretch your budget without sacrificing a social experience, Punto Berro is a fantastic option that lets you explore the best of Montevideo while staying on budget.

Ibis Montevideo Rambla

For travelers seeking a bit more comfort without veering into luxury territory, the **Ibis Montevideo Rambla** offers an excellent mid-range option. Part of the trusted Ibis chain, this hotel sits along the **Rambla**, Montevideo's iconic waterfront promenade, offering easy access to beaches and stunning views of the Río de la Plata.

Rooms at the Ibis are simple but modern, clean, and well-equipped with everything you need for a pleasant stay. It's a particularly great choice for couples, business travelers, or families who want a reliable, comfortable place to stay without overspending. The location, just minutes from the city center, means you can enjoy Montevideo's beaches by day and its cultural landmarks by night. Plus, the hotel's on-site restaurant serves up delicious, reasonably priced meals, saving you the hassle of hunting down food after a long day of sightseeing.

Hotel Iberia

If you prefer a smaller, more intimate hotel experience, **Hotel Iberia** is a hidden gem in Montevideo. Located in **Barrio Sur**, one of the city's more traditional and colorful neighborhoods, Hotel Iberia offers personalized service, cozy rooms, and a great central location—all at a very reasonable price.

While the hotel may not offer flashy amenities, what it lacks in luxury, it more than makes up for in warmth and charm. The staff at Hotel Iberia go out of their way to make you feel at home, offering personalized recommendations and insider tips to help you make the most of your stay in Montevideo. The rooms are clean, comfortable, and perfect for travelers who want an affordable yet pleasant base from which to explore the city.

Smart Budgeting Tips

When it comes to finding budget and mid-range accommodations in Montevideo, there are a few tips that can help you get the most out of your stay. First, consider staying in neighborhoods like **Pocitos**, **Parque Rodó**, or **Barrio Sur**, where you'll find a range of affordable options without compromising on location. These areas are close to the beach, parks, and cultural hotspots, offering a great balance between cost and convenience.

For those on a very tight budget, hostels like **Circus** and **Punto Berro** offer excellent value, especially if you don't mind sharing a room. Not only do you save money, but you also get the chance to meet fellow travelers, which can add a fun, social element to your trip. If you're traveling as a couple or a small group, many hostels offer private rooms, which can be a more affordable alternative to hotels while still giving you some privacy.

For mid-range travelers, hotels like **Ibis** and **Hotel Iberia** provide a step up in comfort while keeping costs reasonable. Booking ahead can often get you better rates, and considering the proximity of these hotels to major attractions, you'll save on transportation costs as well.

Montevideo offers a wealth of budget and mid-range accommodations that let you experience the city's vibrant culture, beautiful beaches, and historic charm without overspending. Whether you're staying in a trendy hostel, a reliable mid-range hotel, or a cozy boutique option, the city's affordable accommodations ensure you can enjoy all that Montevideo has to offer while sticking to your   budget.

From social hostels with lively atmospheres to comfortable mid-range hotels with stunning waterfront views, Montevideo proves that you don't need to spend a fortune to enjoy a memorable and fulfilling stay in this dynamic city.

CHAPTER 4: EXPLORING MONTEVIDEO'S NEIGHBORHOODS

Montevideo is more than just Uruguay's capital—
it's a city with a soul, a patchwork of distinct
neighborhoods, each with its own unique
character, charm, and history. From the vibrant
streets of Ciudad Vieja to the tranquil shores of

Pocitos, exploring Montevideo's neighborhoods is like embarking on a journey through the heart and spirit of Uruguay itself. Each barrio (neighborhood) tells its own story, offering travelers a diverse array of experiences that bring the city to life.

For those who love culture, history, and architecture, the colonial charm of **Ciudad Vieja** is an absolute must. Its cobblestone streets and centuries-old buildings transport you back in time, while the lively markets, restaurants, and museums keep the atmosphere energetic and inviting. If a laid-back, beachside vibe is more your style, you'll find it in **Pocitos** and **Carrasco**, where golden sands meet upscale dining and boutique shopping.

Montevideo's neighborhoods are easy to explore, and whether you're wandering the bustling downtown or relaxing in quieter residential areas, you'll find that each barrio has something special to offer. From the grand plazas of the city center to the artistic enclaves tucked away in unexpected corners, these neighborhoods form the beating heart of Montevideo, reflecting the city's past, present, and future.

In this chapter, we'll take you through Montevideo's most notable neighborhoods, showing you where to eat, shop, relax, and dive into the local culture. Whether you're staying for a weekend or planning a longer visit, getting to know the city's neighborhoods is essential to fully appreciate what makes Montevideo so unforgettable. Let's explore each one, starting with the historic charm of Ciudad Vieja and winding our way through the city's varied and vibrant districts.

4.1 CIUDAD VIEJA (OLD TOWN)

Ciudad Vieja, or Old Town, is the beating heart of Montevideo's history and culture. As the oldest part of the city, it carries with it centuries of stories, architecture, and a vibrant energy that draws visitors from all over the world. Walking through Ciudad Vieja feels like stepping back in time, but with a modern pulse that keeps it lively and relevant. It's a place where the old meets the new, where ancient buildings stand proudly next to trendy cafés and art galleries. Whether you're an art lover, a foodie, or a history buff, Ciudad Vieja has something to offer.

The neighborhood is framed by Montevideo's iconic **Plaza Independencia**, a grand square that acts as the gateway to Ciudad Vieja and holds one of the city's most important landmarks: the **Mausoleum of General Artigas**, Uruguay's national hero. As you step through the towering gateway of the old city walls, known as the **Puerta de la Ciudadela**, you're immediately immersed in the rich cultural fabric that makes this area so special. Cobblestone streets, colonial buildings, and intricate ironwork line the streets, inviting you to take a leisurely stroll and discover the hidden gems tucked into every corner.

One of the most appealing aspects of Ciudad
Vieja is how deeply its history is intertwined with
the present. The **Solis Theatre**, for example, is a
grand, neoclassical building that has been a center
of the arts since the 1850s. Here, you can catch
performances ranging from ballet to classical
music and contemporary theater. For lovers of art,
the **Museo Torres García** is a must-visit,
dedicated to the works of one of Uruguay's most
famous artists, Joaquín Torres García. The

museum offers an intimate look into his legacy and the broader scope of Uruguayan art.

The neighborhood's charm doesn't stop at its historic sites. Ciudad Vieja is also home to **Mercado del Puerto**, a bustling market filled with restaurants and shops. It's the perfect place to indulge in a traditional Uruguayan **asado** (barbecue), with rich, smoky meats sizzling over open flames. The energy here is infectious— locals and visitors alike gather to enjoy a meal, a glass of wine, or simply the buzzing atmosphere.

But Ciudad Vieja isn't just for day trips and sightseeing. As the sun sets, the neighborhood transforms into one of Montevideo's liveliest nightlife spots. Trendy bars, clubs, and live music venues light up the streets, offering everything from traditional **candombe** rhythms to contemporary jazz and electronic beats. Many of these venues are housed in beautiful, historic buildings, which adds a unique ambiance to your night out. Whether you want to dance until dawn or enjoy a quiet drink under the stars, Ciudad Vieja's nightlife has you covered.

The streets themselves often feel like an open-air gallery, with street performers, murals, and art installations dotting the landscape. Wandering through Ciudad Vieja at night is a feast for the senses—you can hear the drums of a nearby **candombe** performance, smell the sizzling meats at a nearby restaurant, and see the colorful lights reflecting off the old buildings.

What makes Ciudad Vieja so special is its ability to take you on a journey through time while still feeling vibrant and alive in the present. It's a neighborhood that preserves Montevideo's past but embraces modern culture, making it an ideal place for any traveler who wants to experience the best of both worlds. Whether you're admiring the architecture, savoring the local cuisine, or soaking in the lively atmosphere, Ciudad Vieja offers an authentic and unforgettable introduction to Montevideo.

For any visitor to the city, starting your exploration in Ciudad Vieja is a must. It's not just a neighborhood; it's a reflection of Montevideo's spirit, a place where history, culture, and modern life coexist in a harmonious and exciting way.

4.2 PUNTA CARRETAS AND POCITOS

Punta Carretas and Pocitos are two of Montevideo's most dynamic and appealing neighborhoods, offering a delightful contrast to the historic charm of Ciudad Vieja. While both neighborhoods embrace a modern, upscale vibe, each has its own distinct personality and rhythm. They offer everything from stunning waterfront views to lively shopping districts, making them must-visit spots for anyone looking to experience the contemporary side of Montevideo.

Punta Carretas: Where Elegance Meets the Coast

Punta Carretas is where sophistication meets coastal beauty. Located on Montevideo's southern shore, this neighborhood is known for its upscale atmosphere and breathtaking views of the **Rambla**, the scenic coastal promenade that stretches along the city's edge. Here, the tranquil sound of waves rolling in from the **Rio de la Plata** serves as a peaceful backdrop to everyday life. For those who love a slower pace, walking or cycling along the Rambla at sunset is nothing short of magical, offering panoramic views of the sea and sky blending into hues of pink and orange.

One of Punta Carretas' most iconic landmarks is the **Punta Carretas Shopping**, a luxurious shopping mall housed in what was once a 19th-century prison. Today, this elegant complex is home to high-end shops, gourmet restaurants, and trendy cafés. It's a perfect place for indulging in some retail therapy or simply relaxing over a cup of **mate** (Uruguay's famous herbal tea) while enjoying the stylish ambiance.

For those interested in culture and history, Punta Carretas also offers a glimpse into Montevideo's more recent past. The **Faro de Punta Carretas**, a historic lighthouse, stands as a symbol of the neighborhood's connection to the sea. It's a peaceful spot for taking in the ocean breeze while learning about the city's maritime heritage.

Punta Carretas is also a fantastic spot for food lovers. The area is filled with some of Montevideo's best restaurants, offering everything from traditional Uruguayan **asado** to international gourmet dishes. With its blend of coastal charm, modern luxury, and fine dining, Punta Carretas offers visitors a taste of the good life in Montevideo.

Pocitos: A Vibrant Beachside Community

Just north of Punta Carretas lies Pocitos, one of Montevideo's most vibrant and cosmopolitan neighborhoods. Known for its beautiful beach, lively atmosphere, and thriving social scene, Pocitos is the place to be if you're looking for a mix of relaxation and excitement. Whether you're soaking up the sun on **Playa Pocitos** or exploring the neighborhood's bustling streets, Pocitos offers a quintessential Montevideo experience that's hard to beat.

Playa Pocitos, with its soft, golden sands and calm waters, is one of the city's most popular urban beaches. On any given day, you'll find locals and tourists alike enjoying the sun, playing beach volleyball, or simply lounging with a book. The Rambla along Pocitos Beach is perfect for a leisurely stroll or a scenic bike ride, with stunning views of the Rio de la Plata on one side and modern, high-rise apartments on the other. The beachside energy is infectious, and it's easy to see why this area has become such a favorite among visitors.

Beyond the beach, Pocitos is a hub of activity. Its streets are lined with cafés, bars, and boutiques that give the neighborhood a trendy, youthful vibe. **Avenida Brasil**, one of the main thoroughfares, is particularly lively, with an array of restaurants offering everything from casual eats to gourmet meals. Whether you're looking for a relaxed coffee spot or a chic restaurant, Pocitos has it all.

The neighborhood is also a hotspot for nightlife, with its many bars and clubs attracting a young, energetic crowd. From sophisticated cocktail lounges to lively pubs, there's always somewhere to unwind after a day of exploring. Pocitos seamlessly blends beachside leisure with urban energy, making it an ideal spot for those who want a bit of everything—whether it's lounging by the water, shopping in chic boutiques, or dancing the night away.

Moreover, Both Punta Carretas and Pocitos offer a glimpse into the modern, sophisticated side of Montevideo. They are neighborhoods where you can enjoy the finer things in life while staying connected to the natural beauty of the coastline. Whether you're strolling the Rambla, enjoying a gourmet meal, or lounging on the beach, these areas provide a perfect balance of elegance, relaxation, and fun.

Visitors to Montevideo in 2025 will find that Punta Carretas and Pocitos are more than just places to stay or pass through—they are destinations in their own right. With their blend of modernity, culture, and natural beauty, these neighborhoods invite you to experience Montevideo at its most vibrant and enjoyable. Whether you're drawn to the upscale charm of Punta Carretas or the lively, beachy vibe of

Pocitos, both areas promise to leave a lasting impression on anyone lucky enough to explore them.

CHAPTER 5:

MONTEVIDEO'S CULINARY

SCENE

Montevideo's culinary scene is a feast for the senses, offering an authentic taste of Uruguay's culture and traditions. The city's food culture is a blend of its rich history, the influence of European immigrants, and a strong connection to local ingredients. Whether you're a foodie looking for a gourmet experience or a traveler eager to try something new, Montevideo promises to satisfy every craving.

In Montevideo, food isn't just about sustenance—it's about community, celebration, and tradition. The people here take pride in their meals, from the simple, comforting dishes to the grand, smoky flavors of an **asado** (barbecue). Dining in this city is more than just eating; it's a way to connect with the culture, to share stories over a meal, and to experience the warmth of Uruguayan hospitality. The culinary experience in Montevideo reflects the city's laid-back vibe, where meals are meant to be savored slowly and enjoyed in good company.

Montevideo's food landscape is diverse, catering to every taste. From traditional Uruguayan cuisine to international flavors, the city offers everything from rustic street food to elegant fine dining. At the heart of it all, however, is a focus on fresh, high-quality ingredients—whether it's the grass-fed beef Uruguay is famous for, the freshly caught fish from the Rio de la Plata, or the farm-fresh vegetables used in local dishes.

Walking through the city, you'll be tempted by the smell of sizzling meat from parrillas (grill houses), the aroma of freshly baked pastries, and the fragrant wafts of herbs and spices from local markets. Whether you're wandering through the bustling **Mercado del Puerto** or enjoying a quiet dinner in a chic bistro, Montevideo's food scene is sure to be a highlight of your visit.

In this chapter, we'll explore the culinary treasures of Montevideo, from the must-try traditional dishes to the best places to eat. We'll dive into the world of **asado**, explore the flavors of Uruguayan street food, and guide you through the city's top restaurants and markets. Whether you're looking for a budget-friendly meal or an indulgent dining experience, this chapter will show you the best that Montevideo has to offer on a plate. Get ready to embark on a flavorful journey through one of South America's most underrated food destinations!

5.1 TRADITIONAL URUGUAYAN DISHES TO TRY

Uruguayan cuisine is a rich tapestry of flavors that reflect the country's heritage, agricultural abundance, and love for simple, yet deeply satisfying meals. In Montevideo, the food tells a story—one of community, tradition, and a connection to the land. Whether you're indulging in a hearty barbecue, tasting freshly made empanadas, or sipping **mate** on a sunny afternoon, there's no better way to understand Uruguay than through its food.

Here are some traditional Uruguayan dishes that you simply must try when visiting Montevideo. These iconic flavors give you a taste of Uruguay's culinary soul, and they're sure to leave a lasting impression   on   your   palate.

1. Asado: The Ultimate Uruguayan BBQ Experience

In Uruguay, **asado** is more than just a meal—it's a way of life. Asado, the country's beloved barbecue, is an essential part of Uruguayan culture. Every weekend, families and friends gather around a parrilla (grill) to cook up a variety of meats over an open flame. The key to a great asado is patience and quality. Uruguayans take pride in their grass-fed beef, known for its rich, natural flavor, and each cut is treated with care.

Whether you're savoring a juicy **entraña** (skirt steak), tender **lomo** (tenderloin), or the flavorful **chorizo** sausage, the smoky, charred flavors of asado will leave you craving more. Be sure to enjoy it with chimichurri, a vibrant herb sauce made with parsley, garlic, vinegar, and oil, that complements the meat perfectly.

For an authentic experience, head to **Mercado del Puerto**, a bustling market filled with traditional parrillas where you can witness the grilling mastery up close. Eating asado in Montevideo isn't just about the food—it's about embracing the relaxed atmosphere, sharing a meal with friends, and enjoying the ritual of barbecue that has been passed down through generations.

2. Chivito: Uruguay's Iconic Sandwich

If there's one dish that defines Uruguay's fast food scene, it's the **chivito**—a massive sandwich that's as delicious as it is filling. At first glance, the chivito may look like an ordinary sandwich, but one bite will prove it's anything but. It's packed with flavors and textures, making it a favorite among locals and visitors alike.

The star of the chivito is a thinly sliced beef steak, grilled to perfection, and piled high on a soft bun. But it doesn't stop there. The sandwich is topped with a variety of ingredients, including ham, bacon, mozzarella cheese, lettuce, tomatoes, and olives. Some variations also include fried eggs, pickles, and roasted peppers. It's typically served with a side of **papas fritas** (French fries), making it a hearty meal.

Chivito is the perfect example of comfort food done right. Whether you're grabbing one at a casual eatery or indulging in a gourmet version at a local restaurant, the combination of flavors in a chivito is nothing short of addictive. Don't leave Montevideo without trying this iconic sandwich—you'll understand why it's a national treasure.

3. Milanesa: A Simple Yet Satisfying Classic

Similar to schnitzel, **milanesa** is a breaded and fried cutlet of beef or chicken, and it's one of Uruguay's most beloved comfort foods. The dish is simple but packed with flavor: thin slices of meat are coated in breadcrumbs and fried until golden and crispy. It's often served with mashed potatoes, salad, or French fries, making it a satisfying and filling meal.

There are also variations of milanesa that take the dish to another level. Try the **Milanesa a la Napolitana**, where the fried cutlet is topped with ham, tomato sauce, and melted cheese—a Uruguayan take on the Italian classic. It's a delicious, indulgent twist that's sure to win you over.

Milanesa is an everyday dish in Uruguay, and you'll find it served everywhere, from casual family kitchens to local restaurants. It's a comforting and approachable meal that gives you a taste of Uruguay's simpler side.

4. Empanadas: Handheld Pockets of Flavor

A visit to Montevideo wouldn't be complete without sampling a few **empanadas**. These golden, flaky pastries are filled with a variety of ingredients, making them perfect for a quick snack or a light meal on the go. Whether you prefer savory or sweet, there's an empanada for everyone.

The most popular fillings are **carne** (beef), **jamón y queso** (ham and cheese), and **pollo** (chicken). The beef empanadas are typically seasoned with onions, garlic, and spices, creating a savory filling that pairs perfectly with the buttery pastry. For those with a sweet tooth, try the **dulce de leche** empanadas—filled with the famous caramel-like spread that Uruguayans adore.

Empanadas are widely available across Montevideo, from street vendors to bakeries, and they're perfect for when you want to grab something quick but still want to experience local flavors. One bite of a warm, freshly baked empanada, and you'll see why this humble dish is so loved by Uruguayans.

5. Torta Frita: Uruguay's Favorite Fried Treat

If you're looking for a little something sweet to accompany your afternoon **mate**, look no further than **torta frita**. This fried dough pastry is a staple in Uruguay and is especially popular on rainy days—locals even have a saying, "Día de torta frita" (fried dough day), for when the weather calls for this comforting treat.

Torta frita is made from simple ingredients: flour, water, and fat, and it's deep-fried until golden and crispy. It's typically sprinkled with sugar or drizzled with syrup for a sweet touch. Whether you're enjoying it with friends or grabbing one from a street vendor, torta frita is a delicious reminder of Uruguay's down-to-earth, communal food culture.

The beauty of Montevideo's traditional dishes lies in their simplicity and the care with which they are made. Uruguayans value quality ingredients and the act of sharing a meal, whether it's a casual snack or a full-fledged asado. Each dish tells a story, and as you savor the flavors of Uruguay, you'll feel a deeper connection to the people, their history, and the warmth that defines this small but vibrant country.

From the sizzling meats of asado to the hearty indulgence of a chivito, Montevideo's culinary scene is a reflection of the country's soul—rich, flavorful, and deeply satisfying. So, pull up a chair, grab a fork, and let these traditional Uruguayan dishes take you on a journey through the heart of Montevideo.

5.2 BEST RESTAURANTS, CAFÉS, AND FOOD MARKETS

Montevideo is a city where food is more than a necessity—it's a celebration of life. Whether you're a dedicated foodie or simply someone who enjoys a good meal, the city offers a delightful array of dining experiences. From upscale restaurants serving gourmet creations to charming cafés offering local flavors, and vibrant food markets bustling with fresh produce and authentic street eats, Montevideo caters to every palate and budget. Let's dive into some of the best spots where you can savor the essence of Uruguayan cuisine.

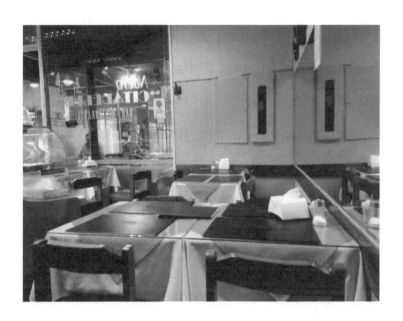

1. Top Restaurants to Experience in Montevideo

Montevideo boasts a fantastic selection of restaurants that showcase both the traditional and contemporary sides of Uruguayan gastronomy. Whether you're looking for a world-class dining experience or a cozy spot for a memorable meal, these restaurants offer something special.

Parrillada El Palenque: Located in the famous **Mercado del Puerto**, El Palenque is a must-visit for anyone looking to experience Uruguay's signature **asado**. Known for its perfectly grilled meats, this restaurant offers an authentic parrilla experience, where the smell of sizzling beef, pork, and chorizo fills the air. The rustic atmosphere, coupled with friendly service, makes it a great place to dive into the heart of Montevideo's barbecue culture. The portions are generous, so be ready for a hearty feast!

La Perdiz: If you're looking for something a bit more refined, **La Perdiz** is a local favorite offering a mix of Uruguayan and international cuisine. With its sleek décor and cozy ambiance, it's the perfect spot for a relaxed dinner with family or friends. Their menu features everything from perfectly grilled steaks to fresh seafood, and their extensive wine list ensures you'll have the perfect pairing for your meal.

Estrecho: For something more contemporary and intimate, **Estrecho** stands out as a hidden gem. Located in the Ciudad Vieja, this small restaurant seats just a handful of people along the counter, offering a minimalist yet flavorful dining experience. The menu is constantly changing to reflect seasonal ingredients, but expect innovative takes on classic dishes using fresh, locally sourced products. It's the perfect spot for foodies looking for something unique.

2. Cafés to Relax and Enjoy Local Flavors

Montevideo's café culture is as much about relaxation and community as it is about the food and drinks. Whether you want to enjoy a cup of **mate**, a local pastry, or simply unwind after a day of sightseeing, the city's cafés provide the perfect setting. These are a few standout spots where you can enjoy a laid-back atmosphere while indulging in delicious bites.

Café Brasilero: One of the oldest cafés in the city, **Café Brasilero** is a historic institution in Montevideo. Located in Ciudad Vieja, it has been serving locals and travelers alike since 1877. With its old-world charm, wood-paneled interiors, and vintage furnishings, it's a great place to step back in time while enjoying a cup of coffee or a refreshing glass of **clericó** (Uruguayan sangria). Try their house-baked **media lunas** (croissants) or **tortas fritas** for a taste of traditional Uruguayan café fare.

Sin Pretensiones: If you're after a more modern café experience, head to **Sin Pretensiones** in the trendy Pocitos neighborhood. With its cozy, laid-back vibe and eclectic décor, this café is a popular spot for locals to gather for coffee, brunch, or light bites. Their menu is fresh and seasonal, offering everything from sandwiches and salads to homemade cakes and desserts. The café also has a charming outdoor patio, perfect for enjoying Montevideo's sunny afternoons.

Philomène Café: Tucked away in the upscale Carrasco neighborhood, **Philomène Café** is a must-visit for lovers of good coffee and elegant pastries. The café's French-inspired menu offers a wide selection of artisanal breads, quiches, and delicate desserts, making it the perfect place for an indulgent breakfast or afternoon tea. The inviting atmosphere and attention to detail make it a favorite among locals looking for a quiet spot to relax.

3. Exploring Montevideo's Food Markets

Montevideo's food markets are where you'll find the freshest ingredients, vibrant local flavors, and a genuine connection to the city's culinary traditions. These markets are perfect for those who want to explore Uruguayan street food, discover artisanal products, or simply soak in the bustling energy of daily life.

Mercado del Puerto: If there's one food market you absolutely must visit in Montevideo, it's **Mercado del Puerto**. This historic market in the Ciudad Vieja is a paradise for meat lovers and a hub for traditional Uruguayan cuisine. With its many **parrillas** (grill houses), Mercado del Puerto is the best place to experience a true Uruguayan asado. The market's lively atmosphere, the smell of grilled meat, and the sound of sizzling steaks make it an unforgettable sensory experience. Grab a seat at one of the open grills, order some **morcilla** (blood sausage) or **entrecot** (ribeye), and enjoy a feast with the locals.

Mercado Ferrando: Located in the trendy Cordón neighborhood, **Mercado Ferrando** is a modern food market with a hip, urban feel. It's the perfect blend of traditional and contemporary, offering a variety of stalls where you can sample local and international flavors. Whether you're in the mood for fresh seafood, craft beers, or vegan-friendly bites, Mercado Ferrando has something for everyone. The market also has a lively bar scene, making it a great place to grab a drink and enjoy Montevideo's vibrant nightlife.

Feria de Tristán Narvaja: For a more eclectic and authentic experience, visit the **Feria de Tristán Narvaja**, one of Montevideo's largest street markets. Held every Sunday, this sprawling market offers everything from fresh produce and homemade cheeses to antiques and books. It's a great place to explore Uruguayan culture through its food. Grab some fresh fruit or try a local street food delicacy like **choripán** (grilled sausage in a bun), and wander through the market stalls for an immersive experience of Montevideo's daily life.

Montevideo's culinary scene is a delightful journey that spans from traditional grills to chic cafés and bustling markets. The city's restaurants offer a blend of local and international flavors, while its cafés provide perfect spots to relax and enjoy the slower pace of life. The food markets, on the other hand, give you an authentic taste of Uruguay's vibrant street food culture and the freshest local ingredients.

No matter where you choose to eat, Montevideo will leave you with memorable culinary experiences, from the smoky flavors of a perfectly grilled steak to the sweet delight of a freshly baked pastry. Each meal in this city is a chance to connect with its culture, savor its traditions, and enjoy the warmth of its people.

CHAPTER 6: CULTURAL AND HISTORICAL HIGHLIGHTS

Montevideo is more than just a coastal city with stunning views—it's a treasure trove of rich history and vibrant culture that spans centuries.

From its colonial past to its thriving arts scene, the capital of Uruguay offers visitors a unique glimpse into the heart and soul of the country. Exploring Montevideo's cultural and historical highlights isn't just about visiting landmarks; it's about understanding the stories and traditions that have shaped the city into what it is today.

Wandering through its neighborhoods, you'll encounter beautifully preserved colonial architecture, grand plazas, and museums that tell the tale of Uruguay's journey to independence. Art lovers will revel in the city's galleries and murals, while history buffs will find a wealth of knowledge in Montevideo's many monuments and historical sites. Even if you're not familiar with Uruguay's history, you'll find yourself drawn into its past through the passion and pride that the locals hold for their heritage.

Whether you're walking through the cobbled streets of the Ciudad Vieja, visiting one of its grand theaters, or simply sitting in a café listening to the rhythms of candombe drums in the distance, Montevideo's cultural essence is something you can feel in the air. This chapter takes you on a journey through the city's most important cultural and historical landmarks, ensuring you leave with a deep appreciation for the city's soul. From museums to markets, each stop reveals a new layer of Montevideo's identity, making this part of your trip an unforgettable experience. If you're ready to dive deeper into the spirit of Montevideo, let's explore the cultural and historical gems that make this city so special.

6.1 MUSEUMS, ART GALLERIES, AND THEATERS

Montevideo's cultural richness is evident in its wealth of museums, art galleries, and theaters, offering visitors a deep dive into the heart of Uruguayan history, creativity, and spirit. Each venue, from the stately museums to the cutting-edge art spaces, tells its own story, reflecting the city's layered past, its evolving identity, and its ongoing artistic evolution. Whether you're an art enthusiast, a history buff, or simply curious, Montevideo's cultural institutions will leave you both enlightened and inspired.

Museums: Exploring Uruguay's Past and Present

Montevideo's museums offer a window into Uruguay's fascinating history and unique culture. From its fight for independence to its contemporary achievements, these museums showcase the country's journey in a way that's engaging and accessible to all.

Museo Histórico Nacional (National History Museum): A must-visit for anyone interested in the roots of Uruguay, the **Museo Histórico Nacional** is spread across several historic homes in Ciudad Vieja, each one filled with artifacts, documents, and exhibits detailing the country's path to independence. As you wander through the beautifully preserved rooms, you'll gain insight into Uruguay's political struggles, its leaders, and the everyday life of its people through the centuries. It's an immersive experience that gives context to Uruguay's current identity.

Museo Torres García: Art lovers will find a haven in the **Museo Torres García**, dedicated to Uruguay's most renowned modernist artist, Joaquín Torres García. Located in the heart of the city, this museum not only showcases his iconic geometric works but also offers a deep dive into his theories on art and culture, which have influenced generations of artists both in Uruguay and internationally. It's a place where you can truly appreciate Uruguay's contribution to the global art scene.

Museo del Carnaval: For a lighter, more colorful experience, the **Museo del Carnaval** celebrates one of Uruguay's most beloved traditions: **Carnival**. This lively museum is filled with vibrant costumes, masks, and photos, bringing the energy of Montevideo's annual carnival parade to life. Visitors can learn about the history of candombe, a traditional Afro-Uruguayan rhythm, and the cultural importance of this unique celebration. It's a joyful experience that provides a deeper understanding of Uruguay's diverse cultural heritage.

Art Galleries: A Window into Uruguay's Artistic Soul

Montevideo is home to a thriving contemporary art scene, with galleries that highlight both local and international talent. From traditional landscapes to avant-garde installations, the city's art galleries showcase the diversity and creativity that defines Uruguay's cultural landscape.

Centro de Exposiciones Subte: For those interested in modern and contemporary art, the **Centro de Exposiciones Subte** is a must-see. Located under **Plaza Fabini**, this underground gallery features rotating exhibitions of contemporary works by Uruguayan and international artists. The space itself is a unique experience, and the art on display often pushes boundaries, challenging visitors to think critically and engage with new ideas. Whether you're into painting, sculpture, or multimedia installations, you'll find something thought-provoking here.

Galería SOA Arte Contemporáneo: Another gem in the city's art scene is **Galería SOA**, which showcases contemporary Uruguayan artists. Known for its cutting-edge exhibits, SOA is a great place to discover emerging talents and explore the evolution of Uruguay's modern art. The gallery's curators are passionate about promoting local artists, making it an excellent spot to experience the current pulse of Montevideo's creative community.

Theaters: The Heart of Montevideo's Performing Arts

Montevideo's theaters are where the city's cultural pulse truly comes alive. From grand, historic venues to intimate performance spaces, Montevideo offers a wide range of theatrical experiences, from classical performances to modern productions, live music, and even tango shows.

Teatro Solís: Undoubtedly the crown jewel of Montevideo's cultural scene, **Teatro Solís** is the oldest and most prestigious theater in Uruguay. Built in 1856, this grand neoclassical building has hosted countless performances, from opera and ballet to contemporary plays and concerts. A visit to Teatro Solís is about more than just the performance; it's about experiencing the grandeur of the theater itself, with its stunning architecture and rich history. Even if you're not attending a show, guided tours of the theater offer fascinating insights into its past, architecture, and role in Montevideo's cultural life.

Sala Verdi: For those looking for something a bit more intimate and experimental, **Sala Verdi** is a great choice. Known for its bold and innovative programming, Sala Verdi showcases modern plays, independent theater productions, and experimental performances. It's the place to be if you want to experience the edgier side of Montevideo's performing arts scene. The cozy atmosphere ensures that every seat in the house feels close to the action, making for a truly immersive theater experience.

Auditorio Nacional del Sodre: Music lovers will not want to miss a visit to the **Auditorio Nacional del Sodre**, Uruguay's national concert hall. This state-of-the-art venue hosts a variety of performances, including classical concerts, ballet, and opera, featuring both local and international artists.

The acoustics are world-class, making every performance a breathtaking experience. It's the perfect place to catch a live symphony or see Uruguay's national ballet company in action.

Montevideo's museums, galleries, and theaters are not just places to visit—they are gateways to understanding the city's identity, its people, and its ever-evolving culture. Each of these institutions offers a different perspective on Uruguay's history and its place in the world today. Whether you're moved by the rich artistic traditions found in its galleries or captivated by the drama and emotion of its theaters, Montevideo's cultural spaces allow you to connect with the spirit of the city in a meaningful way.

By exploring these museums, art galleries, and theaters, you'll gain a deeper appreciation for the creativity, resilience, and passion that define Montevideo. Whether you're immersing yourself in the vibrant past of Carnaval, marveling at the contemporary works of Uruguayan artists, or sitting spellbound in a historic theater, Montevideo's cultural scene will leave you inspired, enriched, and hungry for more.

6.2 COLONIAL ARCHITECTURE AND HISTORICAL LANDMARKS

Montevideo's streets are like pages from a history book, with each step offering glimpses of the city's colonial past. Its beautifully preserved architecture and numerous historical landmarks tell the story of a city shaped by conquest, independence, and the blending of cultures over centuries. For visitors, exploring Montevideo's colonial architecture is not just a journey through buildings, but a way to immerse yourself in the city's identity, where every plaza, statue, and structure carries deep meaning.

Ciudad Vieja: A Walk Through Time

The heart of Montevideo's colonial history is found in **Ciudad Vieja** (Old Town), the oldest part of the city, where narrow cobbled streets lead you to majestic buildings that have stood the test of time. Walking through this district feels like stepping into a different era, where the architecture speaks to the grandeur and complexity of Montevideo's past.

Puerta de la Ciudadela: One of the most iconic remnants of Montevideo's colonial history is the **Puerta de la Ciudadela**, the old city gate. This stone structure was once part of a massive wall that protected Montevideo from invaders in the 18th century. Today, it stands proudly at the entrance to Ciudad Vieja, a symbol of the city's resilience. Passing through the gate feels like stepping into another world, where the bustle of modern life fades, and you're transported back to a time when Montevideo was a strategic military outpost.

Plaza Independencia: Just beyond the Puerta de la Ciudadela, you'll find **Plaza Independencia**, Montevideo's most important square. This grand plaza is surrounded by a mix of colonial and modern architecture, but its central figure is the imposing statue of **José Gervasio Artigas**, Uruguay's national hero, whose mausoleum lies beneath the square. Plaza Independencia serves as a bridge between the old and new, where you can literally stand at the crossroads of Montevideo's colonial past and its present-day dynamism.

Montevideo's architectural landscape is rich with colonial and neoclassical buildings that speak to the city's evolution from a modest colonial settlement to a flourishing capital. As you explore these structures, you'll see the influences of

Spanish, Portuguese, and later European styles that have left their mark on the city's skyline.

Teatro Solís: While not strictly colonial, **Teatro Solís** is a landmark that speaks to the grandeur of Montevideo's architectural evolution. Opened in 1856, this neoclassical theater is one of the oldest in South America and stands as a symbol of Montevideo's cultural aspirations during the post-colonial era. Its stunning facade, with its grand columns and sweeping arches, invites you to marvel at the craftsmanship of a bygone era. Inside, the theater's rich history is palpable, with its grand halls and stages having hosted countless performances over the centuries.

Cabildo de Montevideo: No exploration of Montevideo's colonial architecture would be complete without a visit to the **Cabildo de Montevideo**, located in Plaza Matriz. This elegant building, with its grand arches and whitewashed facade, was the seat of government during colonial times. Today, it houses a museum where visitors can learn about Montevideo's early history, including its role in the fight for independence. The Cabildo is not just a historical landmark; it's a living testament to the city's journey from colonial rule to a thriving democracy.

Iglesia Matriz (Montevideo Metropolitan Cathedral): Just steps from the Cabildo, you'll find the **Iglesia Matriz**, the oldest church in Montevideo, which dates back to 1790. Its colonial baroque facade and tranquil interior are a reflection of the city's early Spanish roots. The church has witnessed centuries of history, from religious ceremonies to political upheavals. As you step inside, the peaceful atmosphere offers a moment of reflection, connecting you to the generations of Montevideans who have passed through its doors.

Monuments of Independence and Progress

Montevideo's historical landmarks are not limited to its colonial past. The city is filled with monuments that celebrate Uruguay's fight for independence and its progress as a nation. These landmarks provide a deeper understanding of the country's national identity and the pride its people take in their history.

Monumento a José Artigas: As mentioned earlier, **José Gervasio Artigas** is a central figure in Uruguay's history, and his legacy is celebrated across Montevideo. The grand statue of Artigas in Plaza Independencia is not just a piece of art, but a symbol of freedom and independence. Beneath the statue lies Artigas' mausoleum, where an eternal flame burns in honor of the man who led Uruguay in its fight for liberation. Visiting this site is a powerful reminder of the sacrifices made for Uruguay's independence and the enduring respect the nation holds for its founding father.

Palacio Salvo: Although built after Uruguay's colonial period, **Palacio Salvo** is one of Montevideo's most recognizable landmarks and a symbol of the city's modernization. Designed in an eclectic style with elements of art deco, gothic, and neoclassical architecture, this towering building was once the tallest in South America. It stands as a testament to Montevideo's ambition and growth in the early 20th century. While it might not be colonial in origin, its presence alongside older structures offers a striking contrast that highlights the city's evolution through time.

Montevideo's colonial architecture and historical landmarks are more than just beautiful buildings—they are the embodiment of the city's spirit and resilience. Each structure, from the grand theaters to the modest stone gates, tells a part of the city's story, a narrative woven with struggles for independence, cultural transformation, and national pride.

Exploring these landmarks allows you to connect with Montevideo's history in a tangible way. Whether you're standing beneath the arches of the **Cabildo**, walking through the gates of the

Ciudadela, or admiring the grandeur of **Teatro Solís**, you are experiencing the living history of a city that has played a crucial role in shaping Uruguay's identity. It's a journey that deepens your appreciation for Montevideo, not just as a modern capital, but as a city with a rich past that continues to influence its present.

CHAPTER 7: MONTEVIDEO
BY THE WATER

Montevideo's coastal charm is one of its most alluring features. Nestled on the shores of the Río de la Plata, the city boasts a vibrant waterfront that beckons visitors to explore its beaches, promenades, and marinas. Whether you're looking to unwind by the water, enjoy leisurely walks, or take part in watersports, Montevideo offers a unique experience shaped by its relationship with the river and the ocean.

In this chapter, we'll take you on a journey along the coast, highlighting the scenic beauty of Montevideo's beaches, the laid-back atmosphere of its waterfront neighborhoods, and the endless activities that await by the water. From sun-drenched afternoons on the soft sands of **Playa Pocitos** to romantic sunsets over the calm waters of **Rambla de Montevideo**, this chapter will give you a glimpse of why Montevideo's coastline is an essential part of life in Uruguay's capital.

Imagine waking up to the sound of waves lapping the shore, stepping outside for a morning jog along the iconic **Rambla**, or savoring fresh seafood while overlooking the glistening waters. For both locals and travelers, Montevideo by the water is more than a backdrop; it's a way of life. Whether you're here for a weekend or an extended stay, the city's waterfront has something special for everyone, blending natural beauty with a warm, inviting atmosphere.

In the following sections, we'll dive deeper into Montevideo's coastal wonders—from the most popular beaches to hidden gems, as well as recreational activities that connect you to the city's maritime culture. Get ready to experience Montevideo like never before, with the water at your side, offering tranquility, adventure, and memories that will stay with you long after you've left the shore.

7.1 BEACHES AND COASTAL PROMENADES

Montevideo's coastline is a treasure trove of beautiful beaches and scenic promenades, offering visitors the perfect blend of relaxation and adventure. Whether you're a sun-worshiper looking to lounge by the water or someone who enjoys long, breezy walks with stunning views, Montevideo's coastal gems are a must-see. The city's beaches and promenades bring both locals and travelers together, creating an irresistible atmosphere of laid-back coastal living.

Playa Pocitos: The Heart of Montevideo's Beach Scene

When you think of beaches in Montevideo, **Playa Pocitos** is likely the first to come to mind. Stretching along the eastern edge of the city, this sandy haven is a favorite among both locals and tourists. Picture soft, golden sands, gently lapping waves, and a lively yet relaxed vibe. On a sunny day, you'll find families picnicking, groups of friends playing soccer, and beachgoers taking refreshing dips in the water. It's the perfect place to spend an afternoon soaking up the sun, whether you're looking to swim or just unwind with a good book.

The **Rambla de Pocitos**, the promenade that runs alongside the beach, is equally charming. Lined with cafes, ice cream stands, and small shops, it's the ideal spot for a leisurely stroll, a bike ride, or even a skate. As you walk, you'll pass joggers and cyclists making their way along the water's edge, enjoying the fresh breeze off the Río de la Plata. In the evenings, the Rambla becomes a social hub, as people gather to watch the sunset or enjoy an outdoor meal with a view.

Playa Ramirez: A More Tranquil Getaway

If you're in the mood for something a little quieter, **Playa Ramirez** offers a more relaxed vibe while still being close to the city center. This smaller beach is located near **Parque Rodó**, one of Montevideo's most beloved parks, making it an ideal spot to pair a beach day with a picnic or a walk through the park's green spaces. Playa Ramirez has calmer waters, perfect for those who prefer gentle waves or are visiting with children.

While it may not have the same bustling energy as Playa Pocitos, Playa Ramirez has its own charm—more space to stretch out, fewer crowds, and a slower pace that invites you to take a moment and breathe in the serenity of the surroundings. The **Rambla near Playa Ramirez** offers picturesque views of the water, with benches along the promenade where you can sit and take it all in.

The Rambla: Montevideo's Iconic Coastal Promenade

No discussion of Montevideo's beaches would be complete without diving into the **Rambla**, the city's 13-mile-long coastal promenade that follows the curve of the shoreline. It's not just a place to walk—it's the heartbeat of the city, a place where life unfolds at a leisurely pace, with people walking, biking, fishing, or simply enjoying the fresh air. The Rambla is one of the best ways to experience the everyday rhythm of Montevideo, as locals take their time, stop to chat, or find a bench to take in the view.

Walking along the Rambla gives you a chance to explore different parts of the city's coastline, from bustling beaches to quieter stretches of shoreline. Every section of the Rambla has its own character: at times, you'll pass through lively areas filled with restaurants and bars, while other parts will offer peaceful, uninterrupted views of the river. One of the most beautiful times to experience the Rambla is at sunset, when the sky turns shades of pink and orange, casting a warm glow over the water.

For a more active experience, many visitors choose to rent a bike and ride along the Rambla, enjoying the sea breeze while covering more ground. It's also common to see groups of friends gathering with thermos and **mate**, the traditional Uruguayan tea, enjoying each other's company as they watch the world go by.

While Playa Pocitos and Playa Ramirez may be the most well-known, Montevideo is full of smaller, lesser-known beaches that are well worth exploring if you have the time. Beaches like **Playa Malvin** and **Playa Buceo** offer more local atmospheres, where you're likely to see Montevideans going about their day rather than hordes of tourists. These beaches have a quieter, more laid-back feel, perfect for those who want to escape the crowds and enjoy a more authentic slice of Montevideo life.

Playa Carrasco, located further east, is another hidden gem that offers a slightly more upscale experience, with chic cafes and restaurants nearby. This area is known for its tranquility, making it a great place to unwind or enjoy a romantic sunset walk along the water.

Montevideo's beaches and promenades aren't just about sand and sea—they're an integral part of the city's culture and lifestyle. Whether you're indulging in a seafood lunch overlooking the water, joining locals for a game of beach volleyball, or sipping mate on the Rambla as the sun sets, being by the water is central to life in Montevideo.

Each beach and promenade has its own vibe, but they all share one thing in common: they invite you to slow down, relax, and enjoy the moment. Montevideo by the water is an experience that will leave you feeling rejuvenated, with memories of sun-soaked afternoons and the gentle sound of the waves as your soundtrack.

7.2 WATERFRONT ACTIVITIES: BOATING AND WATER SPORTS

Montevideo's coastline isn't just for sunbathing and strolling; it's also a playground for anyone with a taste for adventure on the water. With the expansive Río de la Plata and the stunning backdrop of the city, the waterfront offers a variety of exciting activities, from leisurely boat rides to high-energy water sports. Whether you're a seasoned enthusiast or a curious beginner, the city's waterfront is the perfect place to dive into fun.

One of the best ways to appreciate Montevideo's scenic beauty is from the water. The city offers a range of boating options that cater to every taste. For a relaxed outing, consider a **sightseeing cruise** along the Río de la Plata. These tours provide a unique perspective of the city's skyline and coastal landmarks, making them perfect for both first-time visitors and locals looking to rediscover their city.

As you float along, you'll enjoy panoramic views of Montevideo's beaches, marinas, and historic buildings, all while savoring the tranquility of the water.

If you're interested in a more private experience, renting a **boat or yacht** might be the way to go. Many local companies offer rentals for everything from small sailboats to luxury yachts, allowing you to tailor your maritime adventure to your preferences. Whether you're planning a romantic sunset cruise, a family outing, or a celebration with friends, having your own boat gives you the freedom to explore at your own pace and enjoy the beautiful waters of the Río de la Plata.

For those seeking a more adrenaline-packed experience, Montevideo has a vibrant water sports scene that caters to a range of interests and skill levels. From the thrill of windsurfing to the excitement of jet skiing, there's no shortage of ways to get your heart racing on the water.

Windsurfing is particularly popular along the city's beaches. The combination of wind and water creates perfect conditions for this exhilarating sport. If you've never tried windsurfing before, several local schools and rental shops offer lessons and equipment, making it easy to get started. Even if you're an experienced windsurfer, Montevideo's waters provide a challenging yet enjoyable experience.

Kayaking and stand-up paddleboarding (SUP) are also excellent ways to explore the coast. Both activities offer a more serene way to engage with the water, allowing you to glide along at your own pace while taking in the stunning surroundings. Rentals and guided tours are available, making it accessible for all skill levels. Paddleboarding, in particular, is a fantastic way to experience the city's coastline, with the added benefit of a full-body workout.

For those with a taste for speed, **jet skiing** offers a thrilling ride. Renting a jet ski lets you race across the waves, feeling the rush of the wind and the spray of the water. It's an exhilarating way to cover a lot of ground and see the city from a different angle.

Fishing enthusiasts will also find plenty to enjoy in Montevideo. The Río de la Plata is home to various fish species, and local guides can take you to the best spots for a successful day on the water. Whether you're an experienced angler or just looking for a relaxing way to spend a day, fishing offers a peaceful escape with the chance to catch some local fish.

The waterfront in Montevideo is not just a place for activities but also a hub of social life and culture. The marinas and docks are often lively with people enjoying the outdoors, and waterfront cafes and bars offer a great way to wind down after a day on the water. Many establishments have terraces overlooking the water, perfect for enjoying a meal or a drink while soaking in the beautiful views.

Events and festivals frequently take place along the waterfront, celebrating everything from local culture to international sports. Keep an eye out for regattas, sailing competitions, and water festivals that add a lively and festive atmosphere to Montevideo's waterfront.

Tips for Enjoying Waterfront Activities

Safety First: Always wear appropriate safety gear, such as life jackets, especially if you're engaging in activities like boating or jet skiing.

Stay Hydrated: The sun can be intense, so drink plenty of water and apply sunscreen to stay comfortable and protected.

Respect Local Regulations: Familiarize yourself with local rules and regulations regarding water sports and boating to ensure a safe and enjoyable experience.

Check the Weather: Before heading out, check the weather forecast to avoid strong winds or storms that could affect your plans.

Montevideo's waterfront is a dynamic and inviting destination, offering a wide range of activities that cater to every type of water lover. Whether you're seeking relaxation or adventure, the city's coastal offerings provide endless opportunities for enjoyment. Dive in and discover why Montevideo's waterfront is a cherished part of the city's lifestyle and a highlight of any visit.

CHAPTER 8: SHOPPING IN MONTEVIDEO

Montevideo is more than just a city of beautiful beaches and rich cultural heritage; it's also a vibrant shopping destination that offers a blend of local charm and global trends. Whether you're a dedicated shopper looking for the latest fashions, a food lover seeking unique local products, or someone simply wanting to explore bustling markets and quaint boutiques, Montevideo has something for everyone.

We'll guide you through the city's diverse shopping scene, from bustling shopping centers to charming street markets. You'll discover where to find everything from high-end designer goods to handmade crafts, and where you can pick up authentic Uruguayan souvenirs to remember your trip by. Montevideo's shopping landscape is as dynamic as the city itself, reflecting both its modern flair and its rich cultural roots.

Imagine wandering through **Montevideo's premier shopping malls**, where international brands and local designers come together in sleek, modern spaces. Or picture yourself exploring **historic markets**, where the air is filled with the scent of fresh produce, artisanal cheeses, and local delicacies. Whether you're searching for the perfect gift, a unique fashion statement, or simply enjoying the thrill of discovery, shopping in Montevideo offers an experience that goes beyond mere retail therapy.

Montevideo's shopping scene is not only about finding the right items but also about experiencing the city's vibrant energy and discovering the stories behind its products. From chic boutiques in the heart of the city to bustling street fairs that showcase local artisans, the act of shopping here is deeply connected to the city's lifestyle and culture.

In the sections that follow, we'll delve into the best places to shop, offering insights into the city's most popular shopping districts, markets, and stores. We'll also share tips on what to look for, where to find the best deals, and how to navigate the shopping landscape to make the most of your retail adventures in Montevideo. Get ready to immerse yourself in a shopping experience that's as diverse and exciting as the city itself.

8.1 LOCAL MARKETS AND SOUVENIRS

Montevideo's local markets are more than just places to shop—they're vibrant hubs of culture, flavor, and tradition. Wandering through these bustling markets, you'll encounter a sensory overload of sights, sounds, and smells that capture the essence of Uruguayan life. From colorful stalls brimming with fresh produce to artisan shops showcasing handcrafted goods,

Montevideo's markets offer a unique and authentic shopping experience that's hard to find anywhere else.

Exploring Montevideo's Markets

Mercado del Puerto is perhaps the most iconic of Montevideo's markets, and for good reason. Located in the heart of the city's old port area, this historic market is a feast for the senses. As you step inside, you're greeted by the lively atmosphere of vendors grilling succulent steaks, sizzling sausages, and other traditional Uruguayan dishes. The aroma of barbecue fills the air, inviting you to indulge in some of the best local cuisine. The market is also home to a range of stalls selling fresh fruits, vegetables, cheeses, and cured meats, making it a paradise for food lovers.

Beyond the culinary delights, Mercado del Puerto features a variety of shops where you can pick up unique souvenirs. From handcrafted leather goods to colorful ceramics and traditional Uruguayan textiles, there's no shortage of options to bring a piece of Montevideo home with you. Take your time to browse the stalls and chat with the local vendors; they're often eager to share stories about their products and their craft.

Feria Tristán Narvaja is another must-visit market that offers a different kind of shopping experience. Held every Sunday, this sprawling flea market transforms a section of Tristán Narvaja Street into a treasure trove of antiques, collectibles, books, and second-hand goods. Here, you can hunt for unique finds, from vintage vinyl records to old coins and historical memorabilia. The market also features a variety of food stalls where you can grab a bite to eat while you explore.

Souvenirs to Remember

Montevideo's markets are excellent places to find authentic Uruguayan souvenirs that capture the spirit of the city. Here are some top picks:

Mate Cups and Bombillas: No visit to Uruguay is complete without experiencing mate, the country's traditional herbal tea. At the markets, you'll find beautifully crafted mate cups (known as "calabashas") and bombillas (metal straws) that make perfect souvenirs. These items are not only functional but also come in a variety of designs, from simple and elegant to intricately decorated.

Leather Goods: Uruguay is renowned for its high-quality leather products. Look for handcrafted leather bags, belts, and wallets, all made with care and attention to detail. These items are not only stylish but also durable, making them excellent keepsakes from your trip.

Ceramics and Pottery: The markets offer a range of colorful ceramics and pottery that reflect the local artistry. From decorative plates and bowls to quirky handmade figurines, these pieces make for charming and unique souvenirs.

Textiles and Crafts: Traditional Uruguayan textiles, including handwoven rugs and colorful ponchos, are popular among visitors. These items are often made using traditional techniques and can add a touch of Uruguayan flair to your home decor.

Local Wines and Spirits: Uruguay is known for its excellent wines, particularly its Tannat variety.

Many markets have stalls where you can purchase bottles of local wine or spirits like grappa, perfect for bringing a taste of Uruguay back home.

Tips for Market Shopping

Bargain with Confidence: While many prices are fixed, don't be afraid to negotiate, especially in flea markets. A friendly approach can often lead to a better deal.

Cash is King: Many market vendors prefer cash transactions, so it's a good idea to carry some local currency. ATMs are available, but having cash on hand can make your shopping experience smoother.

Stay Hydrated: Markets can be busy and crowded, so make sure to drink plenty of water and take breaks as needed.

Engage with Vendors: Local vendors are often passionate about their products and happy to share their stories. Engaging with them can provide you with insights into the local culture and traditions.

Montevideo's local markets offer a window into the city's vibrant culture and are an integral part of the shopping experience. From savoring traditional foods to discovering handcrafted treasures, these markets provide a rich tapestry of experiences that make your visit memorable. Whether you're hunting for the perfect souvenir or simply exploring the lively atmosphere, the markets of Montevideo are sure to leave a lasting impression.

8.2 MALLS AND MODERN SHOPPING CENTERS

Montevideo's shopping scene extends well beyond its lively markets and quaint boutiques. For those who prefer a more contemporary shopping experience, the city boasts a variety of modern malls and shopping centers that cater to a wide range of tastes and needs. These spaces combine convenience with a touch of luxury, offering everything from international brands to local designer pieces, and from high-end electronics to gourmet dining options.

Discover the Best Malls in Montevideo

Montevideo Shopping is one of the city's premier shopping destinations. Located in the heart of the city, this expansive mall features a wide array of stores, making it a one-stop shop for all your retail needs. Here, you can browse through popular international fashion brands, explore electronics stores for the latest gadgets, and discover unique local boutiques offering everything from jewelry to home décor. The mall also includes a food court with a diverse selection of dining options, from casual eateries to more upscale restaurants, ensuring you have plenty of choices for a meal or a quick snack.

Punta Carretas Shopping is another top-notch destination, located in the trendy Punta Carretas neighborhood. This mall is known for its elegant design and upscale shopping experience. It features a mix of high-end fashion retailers, beauty stores, and specialty shops. If you're in the mood for some leisure time, the mall also houses a cinema, making it easy to catch the latest movies after a shopping spree. The surrounding area is lively, with various cafes and restaurants perfect for relaxing and people-watching.

Shopping Tres Cruces is well-regarded for its convenient location and extensive range of stores. Situated near the Tres Cruces bus terminal, it's an ideal spot for both locals and travelers. The mall's diverse selection includes everything from trendy clothing stores to home goods and beauty products. With its laid-back atmosphere and numerous dining options, it's a great place to unwind after a day of shopping or to pick up any last-minute necessities.

What to Expect at Montevideo's Modern Shopping Centers

Fashion and Accessories: The malls in Montevideo are home to a wide range of fashion retailers, from global brands to local designers. Whether you're looking for the latest trends or classic styles, you'll find plenty of options to suit your taste. Accessories, including bags, shoes, and jewelry, are also well-represented, making it easy to complete your look with stylish additions.

Electronics and Gadgets: For tech enthusiasts, Montevideo's shopping centers offer a variety of electronics stores where you can find everything from the newest smartphones and laptops to home appliances and accessories. The mall's tech sections are often well-stocked and offer competitive prices, ensuring you have access to the latest innovations.

Dining and Entertainment: Beyond shopping, Montevideo's malls provide a range of dining options that cater to all tastes. From fast food to gourmet restaurants, you'll find something to satisfy your cravings. Additionally, many malls feature entertainment options such as cinemas, play areas for children, and occasionally live events, making them a destination for the whole family.

Local Artisans and Specialty Shops: While the malls offer international brands, they also highlight local artisans and specialty shops. These stores offer unique products that reflect Uruguay's culture and craftsmanship. From handcrafted leather goods to artisanal chocolates, these items make great souvenirs and gifts.

Convenience and Comfort: Modern shopping centers in Montevideo are designed with comfort and convenience in mind. With amenities such as ample parking, clean facilities, and customer service desks, shopping here is a pleasant experience. Many malls also provide wheelchair access and family-friendly amenities to ensure that everyone can enjoy their visit.

Tips for Shopping in Montevideo's Malls

Check for Sales and Promotions: Keep an eye out for special sales and promotions. Many malls have regular discounts, and you might find great deals on both local and international brands.

Plan Your Visit: Weekends can be busy, so if you prefer a more relaxed shopping experience, consider visiting during weekdays. Early mornings or late afternoons can also be less crowded.

Explore Nearby Attractions: Malls in Montevideo are often located in vibrant neighborhoods with additional attractions. Take some time to explore the surrounding area, which might include parks, cultural sites, or charming streets filled with cafes and boutiques.

Stay Hydrated and Take Breaks: Shopping can be tiring, so make sure to stay hydrated and take breaks as needed. Most malls have comfortable seating areas where you can rest and recharge.

Montevideo's modern shopping centers offer a blend of convenience, luxury, and local charm. Whether you're looking for high-end fashion, the latest electronics, or unique local finds, these malls provide a comprehensive shopping experience that caters to every need and preference. Explore the best of Montevideo's retail scene and enjoy a day of shopping in comfort and style.

CHAPTER 9:
MONTEVIDEO'S
NIGHTLIFE AND
ENTERTAINMENT

As the sun sets over Montevideo, the city transforms into a vibrant playground where nightlife and entertainment come alive. From lively bars and pulsating nightclubs to cozy theaters and intimate music venues, Montevideo offers a diverse range of activities that cater to every taste and mood. Whether you're in the mood for a relaxing evening with a cocktail in hand or ready to dance the night away, Montevideo's nightlife scene promises something unforgettable for everyone.

This chapter will take you on a journey through the city's after-dark attractions, helping you navigate the best spots to enjoy Montevideo's dynamic and eclectic nightlife. You'll discover where to find the hottest clubs, the coziest pubs, and the most exciting live performances. Montevideo's nightlife is more than just about going out; it's about immersing yourself in the city's cultural rhythms, experiencing local music and dance, and creating memories that will last a lifetime.

Montevideo is known for its friendly and welcoming atmosphere, and its nightlife is no exception. The city's bars and clubs often have a relaxed, yet lively vibe that invites you to unwind and socialize with both locals and fellow travelers. Music plays a central role in Montevideo's nightlife, with venues offering everything from traditional candombe rhythms to contemporary beats. Whether you're looking for an elegant cocktail lounge, a bustling dance club, or a venue showcasing local talent, Montevideo has it all.

In the sections that follow, we'll delve into the must-visit nightlife spots, including where to find the best live music, where to dance the night away, and where to simply relax and enjoy a drink. We'll also explore Montevideo's entertainment options, from theater performances to film screenings, ensuring you have a well-rounded experience of the city's cultural offerings.

Get ready to discover the pulse of Montevideo after dark and enjoy a nightlife experience that's as vibrant and diverse as the city itself.

9.1 BARS, CLUBS, AND LIVE MUSIC VENUES

Montevideo's nightlife is a dynamic tapestry woven with an array of bars, clubs, and live music venues that cater to all tastes and preferences. Whether you're looking to sip a crafted cocktail, dance to the latest hits, or enjoy an evening of live music, the city's nightlife scene offers a vibrant and diverse range of experiences.

Bars: Where to Sip and Socialize

Montevideo's bars are renowned for their relaxed atmosphere and excellent drinks. Here are some top spots where you can unwind and enjoy a great evening:

Bar Facal: Located in the heart of the city, Bar Facal is a historic venue with a timeless charm. It's known for its classic cocktails and an extensive selection of local and international spirits. The bar's elegant interior and friendly service make it a perfect place to enjoy a quiet drink or start a night out.

La Ronda: For a more casual and lively experience, head to La Ronda. This popular spot offers a cozy ambiance with a fantastic selection of craft beers and unique cocktails. The bar often hosts trivia nights and live music, making it a great place to enjoy a drink and some entertainment.

Librería Bar: Combining the charm of a bookstore with the comfort of a bar, Librería Bar is a unique venue where you can sip on cocktails surrounded by bookshelves. The relaxed atmosphere and creative drinks make it a favorite among locals and visitors alike.

Clubs: Where to Dance the Night Away

Montevideo's nightclubs offer energetic environments where you can dance to everything from reggaeton to electronic beats. Here are a few must-visit clubs:

Lola Club: Known for its vibrant atmosphere and excellent sound system, Lola Club is a hotspot for those who love to dance. The club features a mix of local and international DJs and hosts themed parties that keep the energy high and the dance floor packed.

Odeón: If you're looking for a chic and stylish nightclub, Odeón is the place to be. With its sleek design and cutting-edge music, it attracts a fashionable crowd. The club's spacious layout and top-notch DJ sets ensure a memorable night out.

Club Montevideo: This venue combines a relaxed lounge atmosphere with a lively dance floor. It's a great spot for those who want to enjoy a drink and socialize before hitting the dance floor. The club often features live performances and themed nights.

Live Music Venues: Experience the Local Music Scene

Montevideo's live music venues offer a chance to experience the city's rich musical culture. Whether you're into jazz, rock, or traditional candombe rhythms, these venues provide a platform for both local and international artists:

El Club del Cielo: Located in the Ciudad Vieja neighborhood, El Club del Cielo is a renowned venue for live music. It features a range of genres, including jazz, blues, and rock. The intimate setting allows you to enjoy performances up close, making it a favorite among music enthusiasts.

La Trastienda Club: For a more diverse lineup, La Trastienda Club is a top choice. This venue hosts a variety of musical acts, from local bands to international stars. The club's state-of-the-art sound system and comfortable seating make it an ideal place to enjoy live music.

Sala Zitarrosa: Dedicated to showcasing Uruguay's rich musical heritage, Sala Zitarrosa is a cultural gem. It hosts performances of traditional Uruguayan music, including candombe and tango. The venue's cozy ambiance and excellent acoustics enhance the experience, making it a must-visit for anyone interested in local music.

Tips for Enjoying Montevideo's Nightlife

Dress the Part: Many of Montevideo's clubs and bars have a dress code, so it's a good idea to dress smartly. Even casual spots appreciate a neat appearance.

Check the Schedule: Live music venues often have schedules and ticket prices available online. Check ahead to see what's on and book tickets if necessary.

Stay Safe: Montevideo is generally safe, but always keep an eye on your belongings and be cautious of your surroundings, especially in crowded areas.

Embrace the Local Vibe: Montevideo's nightlife is laid-back and friendly. Don't hesitate to strike up a conversation with locals or join in the fun at a lively bar or club.

Montevideo's bars, clubs, and live music venues offer a rich and varied nightlife experience that reflects the city's vibrant cultural scene. Whether you're looking to relax with a drink, dance the night away, or immerse yourself in live music, you'll find plenty of options to make your evenings in Montevideo truly memorable.

9.2 ANNUAL FESTIVALS AND EVENTS

Montevideo, a city brimming with culture and vibrancy, comes alive throughout the year with an array of annual festivals and events that showcase its rich heritage and contemporary flair. Whether you're a culture enthusiast, music lover, or simply looking to experience the local energy, these events provide a unique glimpse into the city's dynamic spirit. From colorful parades to music festivals and culinary celebrations, Montevideo's events calendar is packed with activities that cater to all interests.

1. Montevideo Carnival

Montevideo Carnival is one of the city's most famous and beloved festivals, celebrated with exuberant parades, lively music, and vibrant costumes. Spanning several weeks from late January to mid-February, this carnival is a fantastic opportunity to witness the city's cultural diversity.

The highlights include the "Desfile de Llamadas," a parade that celebrates candombe, a traditional Afro-Uruguayan rhythm, and the "Desfile Inaugural," which features spectacular floats and performances from various cultural groups. The carnival atmosphere is infectious, with street parties and music creating a festive vibe throughout the city.

2. Montevideo Jazz Festival

For jazz enthusiasts, the Montevideo Jazz Festival is a must-attend event. Held annually in early November, this festival attracts top international and local jazz musicians who perform across various venues in the city. The festival's diverse lineup includes everything from traditional jazz to avant-garde performances, providing a rich tapestry of sounds for every taste. Whether you're a long-time jazz aficionado or a newcomer to the genre, the festival offers an exceptional musical experience in a lively and welcoming setting.

3. Festival Internacional de Cine de Montevideo (Montevideo International Film Festival)

Held each year in October, the Montevideo International Film Festival is a cultural highlight for film lovers. This event showcases a diverse selection of films from around the world, including feature films, documentaries, and short films. The festival often includes Q&A sessions with filmmakers, panel discussions, and workshops, making it a great opportunity to engage with the global film community. The screenings take place in various theaters across the city, creating a vibrant atmosphere for movie enthusiasts.

4. Feria del Libro (Book Fair)

The Feria del Libro, or Book Fair, takes place in Montevideo every year, usually in April or May. It's a celebration of literature and culture, featuring a wide range of books, author talks, and literary events. The fair attracts writers, publishers, and readers from across the region and provides a platform for exploring new releases, attending book signings, and participating in literary   discussions.

It's a fantastic event for anyone passionate about literature and the written word.

5. Montevideo Food Festival

For food lovers, the Montevideo Food Festival is a delightful annual event that celebrates the city's culinary scene. Held in various locations throughout the year, this festival features food trucks, gourmet stalls, and cooking demonstrations from renowned chefs.

It's a great opportunity to sample local specialties, such as empanadas and asado, as well as international cuisine. The festival often includes live music and entertainment, creating a lively and enjoyable atmosphere for all attendees.

6. Semana Criolla (Creole Week)

Semana Criolla is an annual event held in late March or early April that celebrates Uruguay's rural traditions and heritage. The festival features traditional music, folk dancing, and rodeo events, offering a glimpse into the country's gaucho culture. Visitors can enjoy traditional Uruguayan dishes, shop for handcrafted goods, and participate in various cultural activities. It's a wonderful way to experience the country's rural roots and vibrant traditions.

7. Montevideo Tango Festival

The Montevideo Tango Festival, held annually in August, is a celebration of Argentina's iconic dance and music. The festival features tango performances, workshops, and dance classes led by talented dancers from around the world. Whether you're an experienced tango dancer or a curious beginner, the festival offers a chance to immerse yourself in this passionate and evocative dance style. The event is held in various venues across the city, providing a lively and romantic atmosphere for tango enthusiasts.

8. Festival de Música de Montevideo (Montevideo Music Festival)

Held in early December, the Montevideo Music Festival is a celebration of various music genres, from classical to contemporary. The festival features performances by local and international artists, including orchestras, bands, and solo musicians. With a diverse lineup of concerts and musical events, the festival offers something for everyone, whether you're a fan of classical symphonies, rock, or electronic music.

Tips for Enjoying Montevideo's Festivals and Events

Check Dates and Tickets: Festivals and events in Montevideo can be popular, so it's a good idea to check dates in advance and purchase tickets if necessary. Some events may require advance booking, especially for popular performances or shows.

Plan Ahead: Consider your interests and plan which festivals or events you'd like to attend. Many festivals have specific schedules, so reviewing the program can help you make the most of your visit.

Dress Comfortably: Depending on the event, you might be on your feet for extended periods or exposed to varying weather conditions. Wear comfortable clothing and shoes, and be prepared for changes in temperature.

Immerse Yourself: Festivals and events are a great way to immerse yourself in local culture. Don't hesitate to participate in activities, try new foods, and engage with locals to fully experience the city's vibrant atmosphere.

Montevideo's annual festivals and events offer an exciting and enriching way to experience the city's culture, music, and traditions. Whether you're celebrating Carnival, enjoying a film festival, or sampling local cuisine, these events provide a vibrant and memorable glimpse into Montevideo's lively spirit.

CHAPTER 10: GETTING AROUND MONTEVIDEO

Navigating Montevideo, Uruguay's vibrant capital, is a breeze with a range of transportation options that cater to every need and preference. Whether you're exploring the historic streets of Ciudad Vieja, heading to the lively neighborhoods of Punta Carretas and Pocitos, or venturing to Montevideo's picturesque coastline, understanding the city's transport options will help you make the most of your visit.

In this chapter, we'll delve into the practical aspects of getting around Montevideo. We'll cover everything from public transportation and taxis to bike rentals and walking routes, ensuring you have all the information you need to move seamlessly through the city. Montevideo's compact layout and efficient transportation network make it easy to discover its many attractions, whether you're here for a short stay or a longer visit.

Explore how to navigate the city's well-organized bus system, the convenience of taxis and ride-sharing services, and the benefits of using bicycles for a more eco-friendly and enjoyable commute. We'll also highlight the best walking routes that let you experience Montevideo at a more leisurely pace, taking in its charming streets and vibrant neighborhoods.

By the end of this chapter, you'll have a clear understanding of the various ways to get around Montevideo, helping you to move with ease and confidence as you uncover the city's many hidden gems and popular attractions. So let's dive into the details of Montevideo's transportation options and get ready to explore this captivating city with ease.

10.1 PUBLIC TRANSPORTATION: BUSES, TAXIS, AND METRO

Navigating Montevideo is straightforward and convenient, thanks to its well-organized public transportation system. Whether you're a first-time visitor or a seasoned traveler, understanding the options available will help you move around the city with ease and confidence. Here's a comprehensive guide to Montevideo's public transportation: buses, taxis, and the metro.

1. Buses

Montevideo boasts an extensive and efficient bus network that covers the entire city and its suburbs. Buses are the primary mode of public transport for both locals and visitors, and they offer a cost-effective way to explore the city.

Coverage and Routes: The bus system in Montevideo is managed by multiple companies, with routes connecting nearly every corner of the city. The buses are numbered, and each route is well-defined, making it easy to figure out which bus you need. Information about routes and stops is typically available at bus terminals and online, and most stops have signs indicating which buses will stop there.

Payment: To use the buses, you'll need a "MONOBUS" card, a rechargeable smart card that can be purchased and topped up at various kiosks and stores around the city. You simply swipe the card on the reader when boarding and alighting the bus. If you don't have a MONOBUS card, some buses also accept cash, but it's advisable to use the card for convenience.

Frequency and Comfort: Buses in Montevideo run frequently throughout the day, especially during peak hours. They are generally comfortable and well-maintained, though they can get crowded during rush hours. It's a good idea to check the schedule ahead of time, as bus frequencies can vary depending on the route and time of day.

2. Taxis

Taxis are a popular choice for those who prefer a more direct and private mode of transportation. They're ideal for short trips, late-night travel, or when you have a lot of luggage.

Hailing and Booking: Taxis can be hailed on the street, especially in busy areas or near hotels and major attractions. Alternatively, you can book a taxi by phone or through various ride-hailing apps available in Montevideo. Many hotels and restaurants also offer taxi services.

Fares: Taxis in Montevideo operate on a meter system. The fare starts with a base charge, and the cost increases with distance traveled and time spent in the cab. Make sure the meter is turned on at the beginning of your ride to avoid disputes over pricing. While taxis are generally affordable, it's a good practice to confirm the estimated fare with the driver safe and comfortable, with drivers who are familiar with the city's layout. It's always wise to use licensed taxis, which are typically yellow with a black stripe. For extra security, you can use ride-hailing apps, which provide additional features like driver tracking and fare estimates.

3. Metro

Montevideo's metro system, known as the "Metró," is a relatively recent addition to the city's transportation network, offering a modern and efficient way to travel across key parts of the city.

Routes and Stations: The metro currently has a single line that connects several important areas of Montevideo, including the central business district and residential neighborhoods. The line is well-marked, and stations are equipped with clear signage in both Spanish and English. The metro is a convenient option for traveling quickly across the city, avoiding traffic congestion.

Payment: To use the metro, you'll need a MONOBUS card, just like for the buses. The card can be used to enter and exit the metro stations. Tickets can be purchased or recharged at metro stations, and some machines accept cash or credit/debit cards.

Frequency and Convenience: The metro operates with a regular schedule, typically from early morning until late at night. It's a quick and reliable option for getting around, especially during peak traffic times when the roads can be congested. The trains are modern, clean, and comfortable, making the metro a pleasant choice for daily commuting or sightseeing.

Tips for Using Public Transportation

Plan Ahead: Before setting out, check the routes and schedules for buses and the metro. Online maps and mobile apps can provide real-time information and help you plan your journey more efficiently.

Stay Aware: While public transportation in Montevideo is generally safe, it's always a good idea to stay aware of your surroundings and keep an eye on your belongings, especially on crowded buses.

Comfortable Travel: Wear comfortable shoes and dress appropriately for the weather, as you might be walking to and from bus stops or metro stations.

Montevideo's public transportation system offers a range of options to suit different preferences and needs, making it easy to explore the city and enjoy all it has to offer. Whether you're hopping on a bus, catching a taxi, or riding the metro, getting around Montevideo is straightforward and convenient.

10.2 BIKE RENTALS AND WALKING TOURS

Exploring Montevideo on foot or by bike offers a unique and immersive experience, allowing you to uncover hidden gems and enjoy the city's scenic beauty at your own pace. With its friendly urban layout and numerous picturesque spots, Montevideo is an excellent city for both walking and cycling. Here's a guide to making the most of bike rentals and walking tours in the Uruguayan capital.

Bike Rentals

Montevideo has embraced cycling as a sustainable and enjoyable way to get around, with several bike rental options available throughout the city. Renting a bike is a fantastic way to explore the city's diverse neighborhoods, parks, and waterfronts.

Rental Services: Numerous bike rental services cater to both locals and tourists. You can find rental shops in popular areas like Ciudad Vieja, Pocitos, and along the Rambla. Many of these shops offer a range of bikes, from standard city bikes to more specialized options like mountain bikes or e-bikes.

Cost and Duration: Bike rentals are typically quite affordable. You can rent a bike for a few hours, a full day, or even longer, depending on your needs. Some rental services offer discounts for longer-term rentals or for booking in advance.

Bike Paths and Routes: Montevideo features an extensive network of bike lanes and paths, making it easy to navigate the city safely. The Rambla, a scenic coastal promenade, is particularly popular among cyclists, offering beautiful views of the coastline. Additionally, the city's parks and green spaces provide pleasant routes for leisurely rides.

Safety Tips: Helmets are usually provided with bike rentals, and it's a good idea to wear one for safety. Make sure to familiarize yourself with local traffic rules and bike lane regulations. Also, keep your bike secure by using the provided locks when you're not riding.

Walking Tours

Walking tours are a fantastic way to experience the essence of Montevideo, allowing you to soak in the city's atmosphere and uncover its rich history and culture up close.

Self-Guided Tours: If you prefer exploring at your own pace, self-guided walking tours are a great option. You can use maps and guides available online or at tourist information centers to create your own route. Popular walking routes include the historic streets of Ciudad Vieja, the vibrant area of El Mercado del Puerto, and the scenic Rambla.

Guided Walking Tours: For a more structured experience, consider joining a guided walking tour. These tours are led by knowledgeable locals who can provide insights into Montevideo's history, culture, and architecture. Tours may focus on specific themes such as historical landmarks, street art, or culinary experiences. Joining a guided tour can also be a great way to meet fellow travelers and get personalized recommendations.

Points of Interest: Walking tours often cover a variety of attractions. Highlights might include the impressive architecture of the Solis Theatre, the lively Plaza Independencia, the charming Mercado del Puerto, and the picturesque parks and gardens scattered throughout the city.

Comfort and Preparation: Wear comfortable walking shoes and dress for the weather, as you'll be on your feet for extended periods. Carry a bottle of water, sunscreen, and a hat if you're exploring under the sun. It's also a good idea to have a map or smartphone with you to help navigate.

Benefits of Biking and Walking

Flexibility: Both biking and walking offer flexibility in your itinerary. You can easily adjust your plans and spend more time at places that catch your interest.

Eco-Friendly: Choosing to bike or walk instead of driving or taking public transportation is a more sustainable choice, reducing your carbon footprint and contributing to a cleaner environment.

Health and Well-Being: Cycling and walking are excellent forms of exercise, helping you stay active while you explore. They also provide a refreshing break from more traditional forms of sightseeing.

Montevideo's bike rentals and walking tours provide wonderful opportunities to explore the city in a more intimate and engaging way. Whether you're pedaling along the coast or strolling through its lively neighborhoods, you'll experience the city's charm and vibrancy in a way that's both enjoyable and rewarding. So grab a bike or put on your walking shoes, and get ready to discover Montevideo's many delights at your own pace.

CHAPTER 11: DAY TRIPS FROM MONTEVIDEO

Montevideo, with its vibrant culture, stunning coastline, and rich history, is a fantastic destination in its own right. But the Uruguayan capital is also perfectly positioned for a range of exciting day trips that offer a deeper exploration of the region's natural beauty and cultural heritage. Whether you're looking to escape the city for a day or simply want to add some variety to your itinerary, there's a wealth of nearby destinations waiting to be discovered.

In this chapter, we'll guide you through the top day trips you can take from Montevideo. From charming coastal towns to picturesque vineyards, historic sites, and breathtaking landscapes, each destination offers its own unique experience. You'll find everything you need to plan your excursions, including practical tips on how to get there, what to see, and how to make the most of your time away from the city.

We'll start with the coastal town of Punta del Este, known for its glamorous beaches and lively nightlife. Then, we'll explore the quaint town of Colonia del Sacramento, a UNESCO World Heritage site with its well-preserved colonial architecture and charming streets. For those interested in wine, we'll introduce you to the nearby wine regions, where you can enjoy tours and tastings at some of Uruguay's best vineyards. Lastly, we'll touch on natural wonders like the stunning landscapes of the Cuchilla Grande and the serene beauty of the Santa Teresa National Park.

By the end of this chapter, you'll have a comprehensive understanding of the various day trip options available from Montevideo. Whether you're a history buff, a nature lover, or simply looking to relax and unwind, these nearby destinations will provide a refreshing complement to your Montevideo experience. So, pack your bags, grab your camera, and get ready to discover the diverse and captivating regions surrounding Uruguay's bustling capital.

11.1 COLONIA DEL SACRAMENTO

Nestled along the banks of the Rio de la Plata, just a short drive from Montevideo, lies Colonia del Sacramento—a charming gem that promises to transport you back in time. This picturesque town, a UNESCO World Heritage site, offers a delightful blend of historic ambiance and natural beauty, making it an ideal destination for a day trip from the Uruguayan capital.

Colonia del Sacramento is renowned for its well-preserved colonial architecture and cobblestone streets, which echo with the stories of its storied past. Founded in 1680 by the Portuguese and later taken over by the Spanish, the town has a rich and complex history that's evident in its architecture and layout. As you wander through its narrow streets, you'll encounter a captivating mix of Portuguese and Spanish influences, reflected in the colorful façades, wrought-iron balconies, and quaint plazas.

At the heart of Colonia del Sacramento is its Historic Quarter, a labyrinth of charming streets lined with colonial buildings that have been lovingly restored. The area is a delight to explore on foot, offering countless photo opportunities and a genuine sense of stepping back in time. Key landmarks include the Plaza Mayor, which served as the town's central square, and the Basilica del Santísimo Sacramento, one of the oldest churches in Uruguay.

For a taste of Colonia's maritime history, head to the iconic lighthouse, which dates back to the 19th century. Climb to the top for panoramic views of the town and the Rio de la Plata. Nearby, you'll find the remains of the old fortifications and military buildings, which provide insight into the town's strategic importance during colonial times.

Beyond its historical charm, Colonia del Sacramento offers a range of cultural and culinary experiences that will enrich your visit. The town is home to several museums that delve into its past and present. The Museo Portugués and Museo del Indio are excellent places to learn about the Portuguese influence and indigenous cultures. The Museo Municipal offers insights into local history and culture, with exhibits ranging from colonial artifacts to contemporary art.

The town boasts a selection of delightful eateries where you can savor traditional Uruguayan dishes. Enjoy a leisurely lunch at one of the town's charming restaurants or cafés, where you can try local specialties such as grilled meats, fresh seafood, and delicious pastries. Pair your meal with a glass of Uruguayan wine or a refreshing local beverage.

Colonia del Sacramento is not just about history; it also offers plenty of opportunities to relax and enjoy its natural beauty. Take a leisurely stroll along the riverside promenade, which offers stunning views of the Rio de la Plata. The gentle breeze and picturesque scenery make it an ideal spot for a peaceful walk or a relaxing break.

The town is dotted with lovely parks and green spaces where you can unwind. Spend some time in the Plaza Mayor or the Parque Ferrando, enjoying the lush surroundings and the serene atmosphere. Don't forget to explore the local shops and markets for unique souvenirs. From handcrafted goods to local artisanal products, you'll find plenty of treasures to remember your visit by.

Colonia del Sacramento is easily accessible from Montevideo by car or bus. The drive takes approximately 2.5 hours, while buses offer a comfortable and convenient option. There are also ferry services available if you prefer a scenic ride across the Rio de la Plata. The town is charming year-round, but the best times to visit are during the spring and fall when the weather is pleasant and the crowds are smaller. Summer can be quite busy, especially with tourists, while winter offers a quieter experience.

Colonia del Sacramento is a destination that beautifully blends history, culture, and natural beauty. Its cobblestone streets, historic sites, and charming atmosphere make it a perfect day trip from Montevideo, offering a glimpse into Uruguay's rich heritage and providing a memorable escape from the city. So, whether you're a history enthusiast, a culture seeker, or simply looking for a picturesque retreat, Colonia del Sacramento is sure to captivate and enchant you.

11.2 PUNTA DEL ESTE

A short drive from Montevideo, Punta del Este stands as Uruguay's premier beach destination, offering a dazzling blend of sun, sea, and sophistication. This renowned coastal city, often dubbed the "Saint-Tropez of South America," is celebrated for its stunning beaches, vibrant nightlife, and upscale lifestyle, making it an irresistible day trip for anyone visiting the Uruguayan capital.

Punta del Este's allure starts with its beautiful beaches, which stretch for miles along the Atlantic coast. Playa Brava, with its iconic sculpture, "La Mano," is famous for its powerful waves and is a favorite among surfers and beachgoers alike. Its dramatic coastline and bustling boardwalk offer the perfect backdrop for sunbathing, people-watching, or just taking in the panoramic views of the ocean. In contrast, Playa Mansa, located on the opposite side of the peninsula, is known for its calm waters, making it ideal for families and those looking for a more relaxed beach experience.

Here, you can enjoy gentle swims or simply

lounge by the shore while soaking up the tranquil surroundings.

Beyond the beaches, Punta del Este boasts a thriving cultural scene. The city is home to a variety of art galleries and cultural institutions. The Museo Ralli, located in the Beverly Hills area, showcases contemporary Latin American art in a stunning setting, while the Casa Pueblo, the unique home and workshop of artist Carlos Páez Vilaró, offers an insight into the creative genius behind its striking architecture and eclectic art collection. This blend of culture and creativity enriches the Punta del Este experience, providing visitors with both visual and intellectual stimulation.

For those seeking vibrant nightlife, Punta del Este is a city that never sleeps. As the sun sets, the city transforms into a lively hub of activity. The

Marina, with its upscale restaurants and chic bars, becomes a hotspot for dining and socializing. The nightlife here is as diverse as it is dynamic— whether you're in the mood for a high-energy nightclub, a laid-back beach bar, or a cozy jazz club, Punta del Este has something to offer. During the summer months, the city hosts a range of events, from music festivals to glamorous parties, ensuring that there's always something exciting happening after dark.

Punta del Este is also known for its luxury shopping and dining options. The city's shopping scene features a mix of high-end boutiques and artisan markets where you can find everything from designer clothing to unique local crafts. When it comes to dining, Punta del Este offers an array of choices, from sophisticated seafood restaurants with ocean views to charming cafés serving   delicious   local   cuisine.

Dining here is not just about the food; it's an experience that combines great flavors with stunning settings.

For those interested in exploring beyond the city, Punta del Este offers several interesting excursions. The nearby Isla Gorriti, accessible by a short boat ride, is a peaceful retreat with beautiful beaches and hiking trails. Alternatively, the town of La Barra, known for its bohemian vibe and picturesque scenery, is worth a visit for a taste of a more relaxed coastal atmosphere.

Traveling to Punta del Este from Montevideo is straightforward and convenient. The drive takes about two hours, offering a scenic journey along Uruguay's beautiful coastline. Alternatively, bus services are available for a comfortable and easy transfer. Whether you're visiting for a day or extending your stay, Punta del Este promises a memorable experience filled with sun, culture, and excitement.

Punta del Este is a must-visit destination for anyone exploring Uruguay. Its pristine beaches, vibrant nightlife, cultural attractions, and luxurious amenities offer a perfect blend of relaxation and entertainment. So pack your sunscreen, prepare for a day of indulgence, and let Punta del Este enchant you with its charm and elegance.

CHAPTER 12: PRACTICAL TIPS FOR TRAVELERS

When venturing to a new city, having a set of practical tips at your disposal can make all the difference in ensuring a smooth and enjoyable experience. Montevideo, with its vibrant culture, stunning waterfronts, and welcoming locals, is no exception. As you plan your trip to this dynamic

Uruguayan capital, it's essential to be well-prepared to navigate various aspects of your journey with ease.

In this chapter, we'll dive into essential practical tips that will help you make the most of your time in Montevideo. From understanding the financial nuances and language differences to navigating health and safety considerations, these insights will equip you with the knowledge you need to travel confidently and comfortably.

We'll explore everything from handling money matters—like currency exchange and tipping etiquette—to mastering the local language and cultural nuances. We'll also cover important aspects of travel health, safety, and insurance, ensuring that you're prepared for any situation that may arise during your stay.

With these practical tips, you'll be ready to embrace all that Montevideo has to offer, from its rich historical landmarks and bustling markets to its picturesque beaches and lively nightlife. So, let's embark on this journey together, armed with the knowledge that will turn your visit to Montevideo into a truly memorable adventure.

12.1 MONEY MATTERS, LANGUAGE, AND TIPPING ETIQUETTE

When heading to Montevideo, being prepared for financial transactions, language differences, and tipping practices can make your trip smoother and more enjoyable. Let's break down what you need to know about money, language, and tipping to ensure you have a seamless experience in Uruguay's vibrant capital.

Money Matters:

Montevideo's official currency is the Uruguayan peso (UYU). While many places in the city accept major credit and debit cards, having some cash on hand is practical for smaller purchases, local markets, and places that may not take cards. You'll find ATMs throughout the city, and currency exchange services are readily available at banks and dedicated exchange offices.

Before you travel, it's a good idea to check the current exchange rate and maybe even exchange a small amount of money in advance. This way, you'll be ready for your initial expenses upon arrival. In Montevideo, it's common to use cash for public transportation, taxis, and tips, so having a mix of cash and card options will serve you well.

Language:

Spanish is the official language of Uruguay, and while many people in Montevideo, especially in tourist areas, speak some English, learning a few key Spanish phrases can greatly enhance your experience. Simple expressions like "Hola" (Hello), "Gracias" (Thank you), and "Por favor" (Please) are not only polite but can help you navigate interactions with locals more comfortably.

If you're not fluent in Spanish, don't worry—most people will appreciate your efforts to communicate in their language. For more complex conversations, having a translation app handy can be a lifesaver. In restaurants, hotels, and shops, English is commonly spoken, so you shouldn't have too much trouble, but making an effort to speak Spanish can enrich your travel experience and help you connect more deeply with the local culture.

Tipping Etiquette:

Tipping in Montevideo is customary but not obligatory. In restaurants, it's standard to leave a tip of around 10% of the bill if service is not included. Check your bill to see if a service charge has already been added; if so, there's no need to tip extra unless the service was exceptional.

For taxis, rounding up the fare to the nearest convenient amount is common practice. In cafes and bars, leaving small change or rounding up the bill is appreciated. If you receive outstanding service, feel free to give a bit more as a gesture of gratitude.

Overall, being aware of these financial and cultural norms will help you navigate Montevideo with ease. It's all about blending in smoothly with local customs while ensuring that you're prepared for various situations that might arise. With a bit of preparation, you can enjoy everything Montevideo has to offer without any hiccups.

12.2 HEALTH, SAFETY, AND TRAVEL INSURANCE

Traveling to Montevideo is an exciting adventure, and being prepared for health, safety, and insurance matters will help ensure that your trip goes smoothly. Here's a comprehensive guide to help you stay healthy, safe, and covered during your visit to Uruguay's charming capital.

Health:

Montevideo is a clean and relatively safe city, but it's always smart to take some basic health precautions. The tap water in Montevideo is generally safe to drink, so you don't need to worry about buying bottled water unless you prefer it. However, if you have specific health concerns or dietary needs, it's wise to bring any necessary medications with you. Make sure your routine vaccinations are up to date and consider bringing a small first aid kit with essentials like pain relievers, bandages, and any personal medications you might need.

If you have any health conditions or special needs, it's a good idea to consult with your healthcare provider before traveling. They can offer advice specific to your situation and help ensure you have everything you need for a healthy trip.

Safety:

Montevideo is known for being a safe city, but like in any major urban area, it's important to stay vigilant. Keep your personal belongings secure, and be mindful of your surroundings, especially in crowded places or when using public transportation. Avoid displaying valuable items such as expensive jewelry or large amounts of cash, and use a money belt or a secure bag to keep your essentials close.

If you're using taxis or rideshare services, opt for reputable companies or apps. In the event of an emergency, local emergency services can be reached by dialing 911. It's also helpful to have a copy of your passport and important documents stored separately from the originals, just in case.

Travel Insurance:

Travel insurance is a wise investment for any trip, offering peace of mind and financial protection against unexpected events. Before purchasing a policy, carefully review what's covered, especially for medical emergencies, trip cancellations, and lost luggage. Make sure the policy provides adequate coverage for the duration of your stay and includes emergency medical evacuation if necessary.

Travel insurance can help cover medical expenses, trip interruptions, or unexpected events like lost or stolen belongings. It's especially useful if you encounter any health issues or travel disruptions during your trip. By investing in travel insurance, you're protecting yourself from potential financial burdens and ensuring that you can handle any unforeseen situations that might arise.

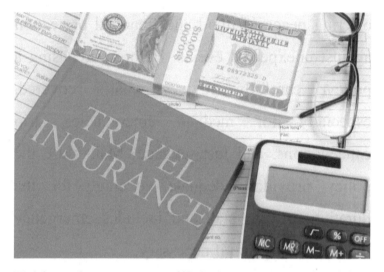

Taking these steps will help you stay healthy, safe, and prepared throughout your time in Montevideo. With a bit of planning and awareness, you can focus on enjoying all the wonderful experiences that this vibrant city has to offer.

CONCLUSION

As you prepare to embark on your journey to Montevideo, Uruguay, remember that this city offers a unique blend of charm, culture, and vibrant experiences that are sure to leave a lasting impression. From its picturesque coastal promenades and historic neighborhoods to its rich culinary scene and welcoming atmosphere, Montevideo is a destination that caters to a wide range of interests and preferences.

Navigating the city with confidence is key to making the most of your visit. Understanding the essentials of transportation, accommodations, and local customs will help you move seamlessly through Montevideo, allowing you to immerse yourself fully in its wonders. Whether you're indulging in traditional Uruguayan dishes, exploring cultural landmarks, or simply relaxing by the waterfront, your time in Montevideo promises to be memorable.

As you explore Montevideo's neighborhoods, appreciate the city's historical depth, and engage in its dynamic nightlife, keep in mind the practical tips on health, safety, and travel insurance. Being well-prepared ensures that you can focus on enjoying your adventure without unnecessary stress. Embrace the local culture, connect with its people, and take in the beauty and vibrancy that define Montevideo.

This guide is designed to help you experience Montevideo to the fullest, providing you with the tools and insights needed for a successful and enjoyable trip. Whether you're a first-time visitor or returning to rediscover the city's delights, may your journey be filled with discovery, joy, and unforgettable moments.

Montevideo awaits with open arms, and as you explore its streets and soak in its atmosphere, you'll find that the city's warmth and character will make you feel right at home. Safe travels, and enjoy every moment of your Montevideo adventure!

Made in United States
Troutdale, OR
12/19/2024

26952524R00159